The Nashville
Book of Dates

ville

Book of Dates

Adventures, Escapes, and Secret Spots

EDEN DAWN
ASHOD SIMONIAN

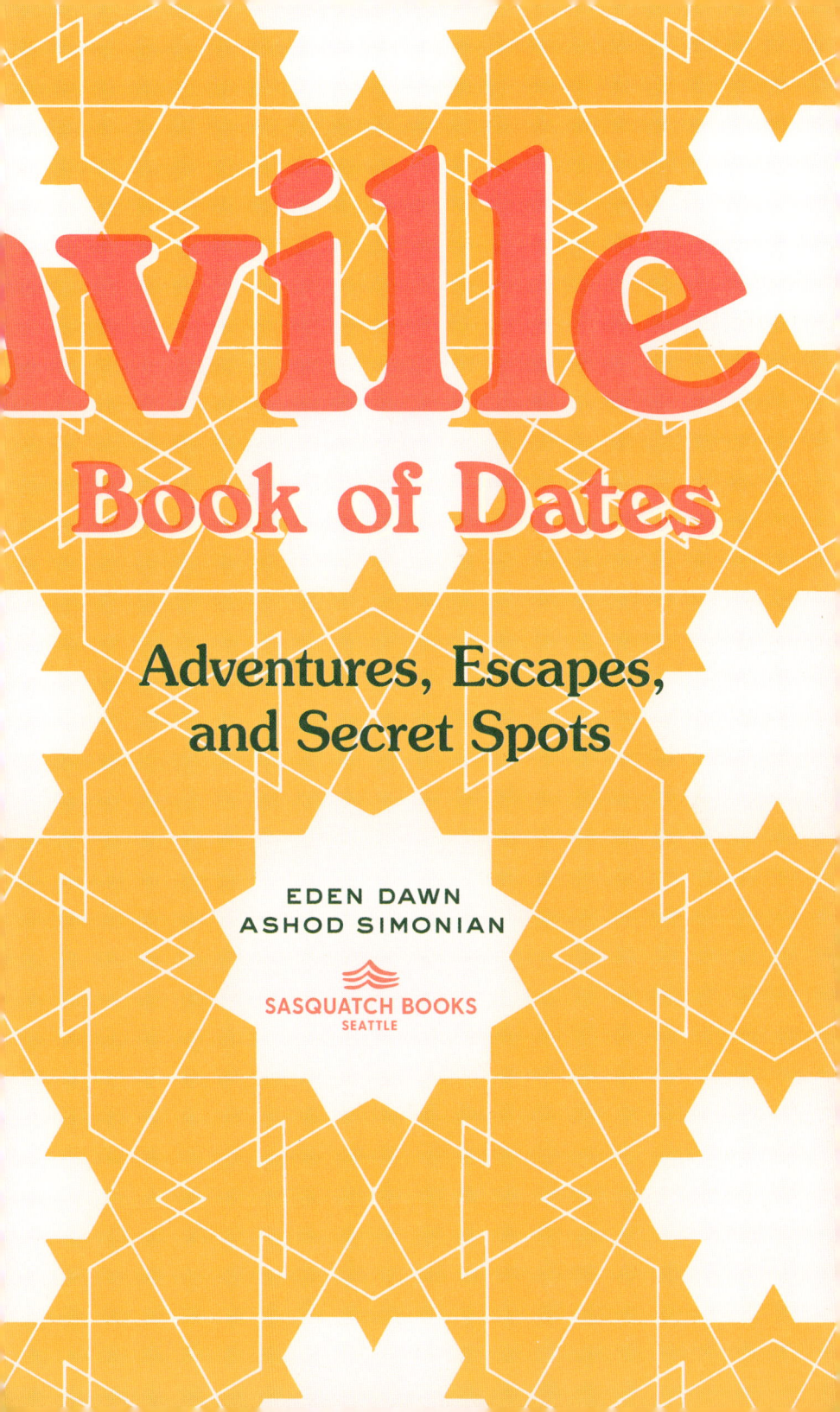

SASQUATCH BOOKS
SEATTLE

Printed in China

SASQUATCH BOOKS with colophon is a registered trademark of Blue Star Press, LLC

29 28 27 26 25   9 8 7 6 5 4 3 2 1

The authorized representative in the EU for product safety and compliance is Authorised Rep Compliance Ltd, Ground Floor, 71 Lower Baggot Street, Dublin D02 P593, Ireland. www.arccompliance.com

Editor: Jill Saginario
Production editor: Peggy Gannon
Production designer: Tony Ong
Illustrator: Ashod Simonian

Library of Congress Cataloging-in-Publication Data
Names: Dawn, Eden author | Simonian, Ashod author
Title: The Nashville book of dates : adventures, escapes, and secret spots / Eden Dawn and Ashod Simonian.
Description: Seattle : Sasquatch Books, [2025] | Summary: "Stylish, cheeky, and above all, curated, The Nashville Book of Dates is the ultimate encyclopedia of cool places for Nashvillains (and visitors). Identifiers: LCCN 2024062263 | ISBN 9781632175779 paperback | ISBN 9781632175700 epub
Subjects: LCSH: Nashville (Tenn.)--Guidebooks | Nashville (Tenn.)--Description and travel | Dating (Social customs)--Tennessee--Nashville
Classification: LCC F444.N23 D39 2025 | DDC 917.68/5504--dc23/eng/20250424
LC record available at https://lccn.loc.gov/2024062263

ISBN: 978-1-63217-577-9

Sasquatch Books
1325 Fourth Avenue, Suite 1025
Seattle, WA 98101

SasquatchBooks.com

To Dolly Parton.
We will always love you.

ZONE 1

In Town

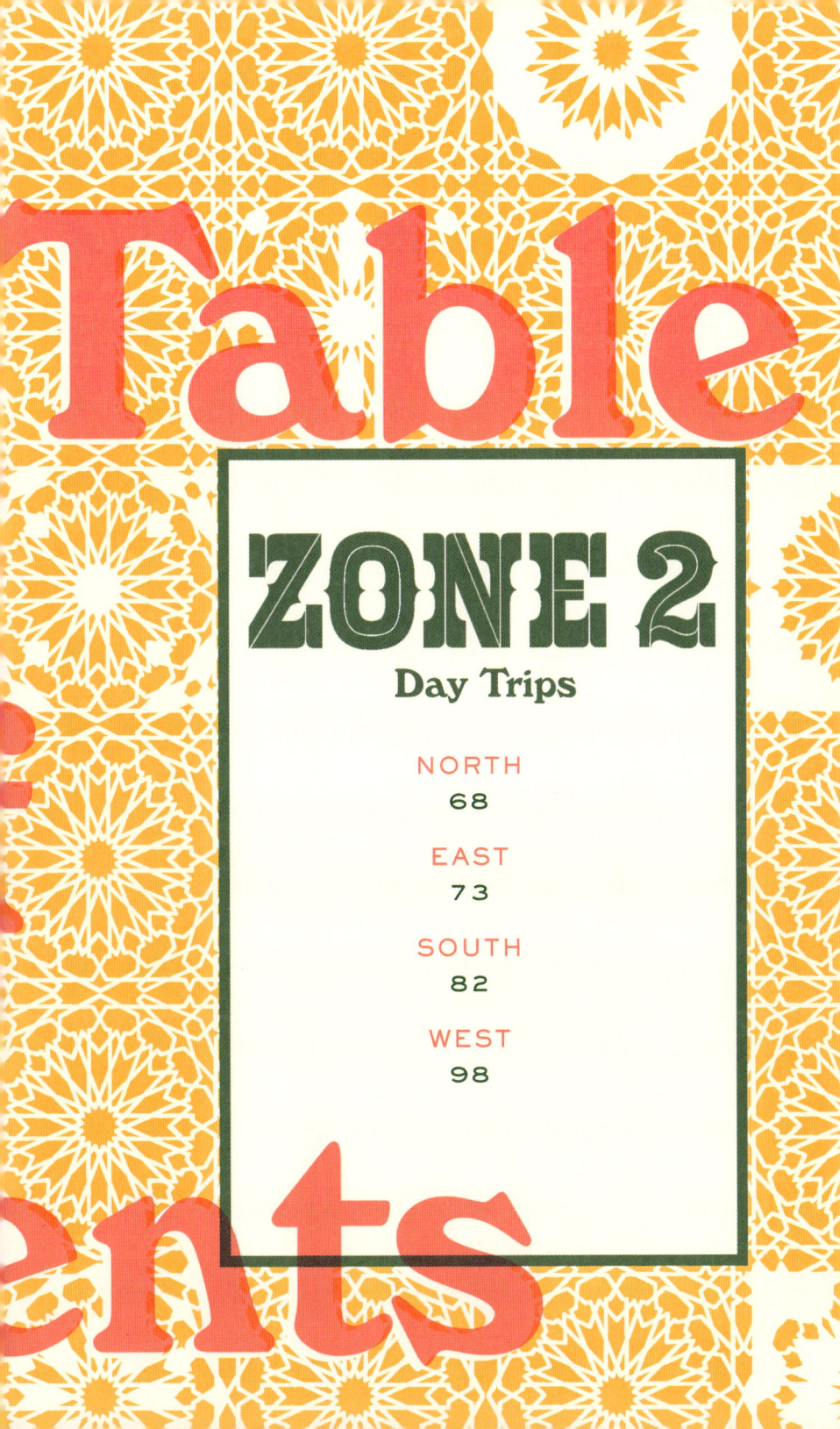

ZONE 2

Day Trips

NORTH
68

EAST
73

SOUTH
82

WEST
98

ZONE 3

Overnighters

An imperfect but, hopefully, helpful map

LOUISVILLE

MAMMOTH CAVE

• KENTUCKY LAKE

NASHVILLE

FRANKLIN •

• MEMPHIS

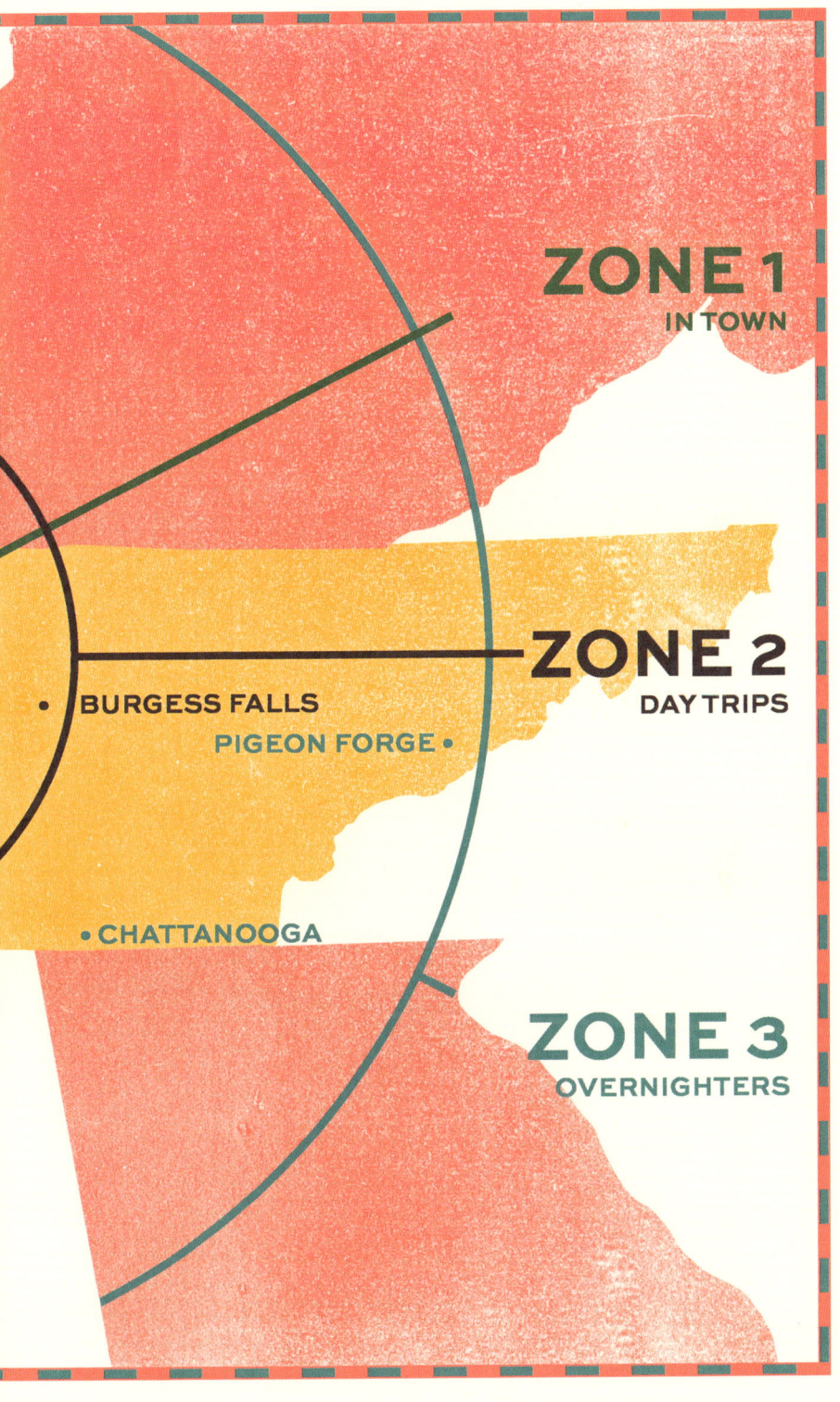

ZONE 1
IN TOWN

ZONE 2
DAY TRIPS

• BURGESS FALLS
PIGEON FORGE •

• CHATTANOOGA

ZONE 3
OVERNIGHTERS

Introduction

Now that we have three of these *Book of Dates* under our belts, people often ask us if we are relationship experts. The answer is a resounding NO! We like to think of ourselves as fun experts. "Dates" is the loose term we've given to making intentional plans to have fun, whether it be with a romantic partner, a group of friends, your visiting family members, or even by yourself. We think making out is fun, so that is highly encouraged on any of these dates—obviously with romantic partners (unless you have a very fun group of friends). Hearing stories about how we've helped people fall in love will never cease to blow our minds. Sharing and spreading love has become a life mission for both of us in everything we do. And we do a lot!

In 2023, Eden won a Guinness World Record for producing the longest drag show in history, while Ashod was busy building a boutique perfume brand called Imaginary Authors. We thought we'd be done with this series after traversing every corner of the Pacific Northwest for *The Portland Book of Dates* and its follow-up, *The Seattle Book of Dates*. When our publisher asked us if we'd like to give another city a shot, our initial thought was, "What right do we have to write a book about a city we don't live in?" But even at home, every good date starts with research. We scour the internet, pore through publications, read every review possible, and spend way too much time on TikTok.

From Ashod's days of touring in rock bands, we have friends spread across the country, and if anybody knows where to grab a life-changing meal (spoiler alert: Peninsula) or catch an amazing show (shhhh: The Basement), it's musicians. When we began to convince ourselves that we might be able to pull off something special, we checked in with our Nashville buds, asking if Plaza Mariachi was worth the drive out on Nolensville Pike or if sipping wine with your feet in the creek at Wines in the Fork was as magical as it sounded. To our utter shock and surprise, these were places that our friends had never heard of. We booked plane tickets immediately and crisscrossed the state in search of the cozy, the dazzling, and the downright kitsch.

The synchronized fireflies brought us back to Gatlinburg, a place we first visited when Ashod surprised Eden on her thirty-fifth birthday with a trip to Dollywood (complete with friends from all over popping out from around every corner). We sipped on tropical cocktails on the Cumberland at Blue Moon Waterfront Grille, late afternoon martinis at Sperry's, and stiff late-night drinks with the regulars at Dino's Bar & Grill. Yeah, our job is a real grind. Having written and released our first book during the pandemic, we know that many of the beloved haunts immortalized within will not be with us forever. But one way to help ensure these treasures thrive and survive is to show up and support all these wonderful small businesses (Refinery Fragrances), queer neighbors (The Lipstick Lounge), and minority-owned eateries (Vui's Kitchen).

For this reason, we have no qualms about sharing our love for these spots far and wide. And one thing that is never going away is the stunning nature around Nashville and the outlying regions. There's more than enough room for all of us to enjoy a springtime stroll through Cheekwood, a summer float on the Harpeth, a fall drive down the Natchez Trace, or a winter in the snowy Gatlinburg hills.

WE WISH YOU JOY AND HAPPINESS,
BUT ABOVE ALL OF THIS,
WE WISH YOU LOVE.

Eden & Ashod

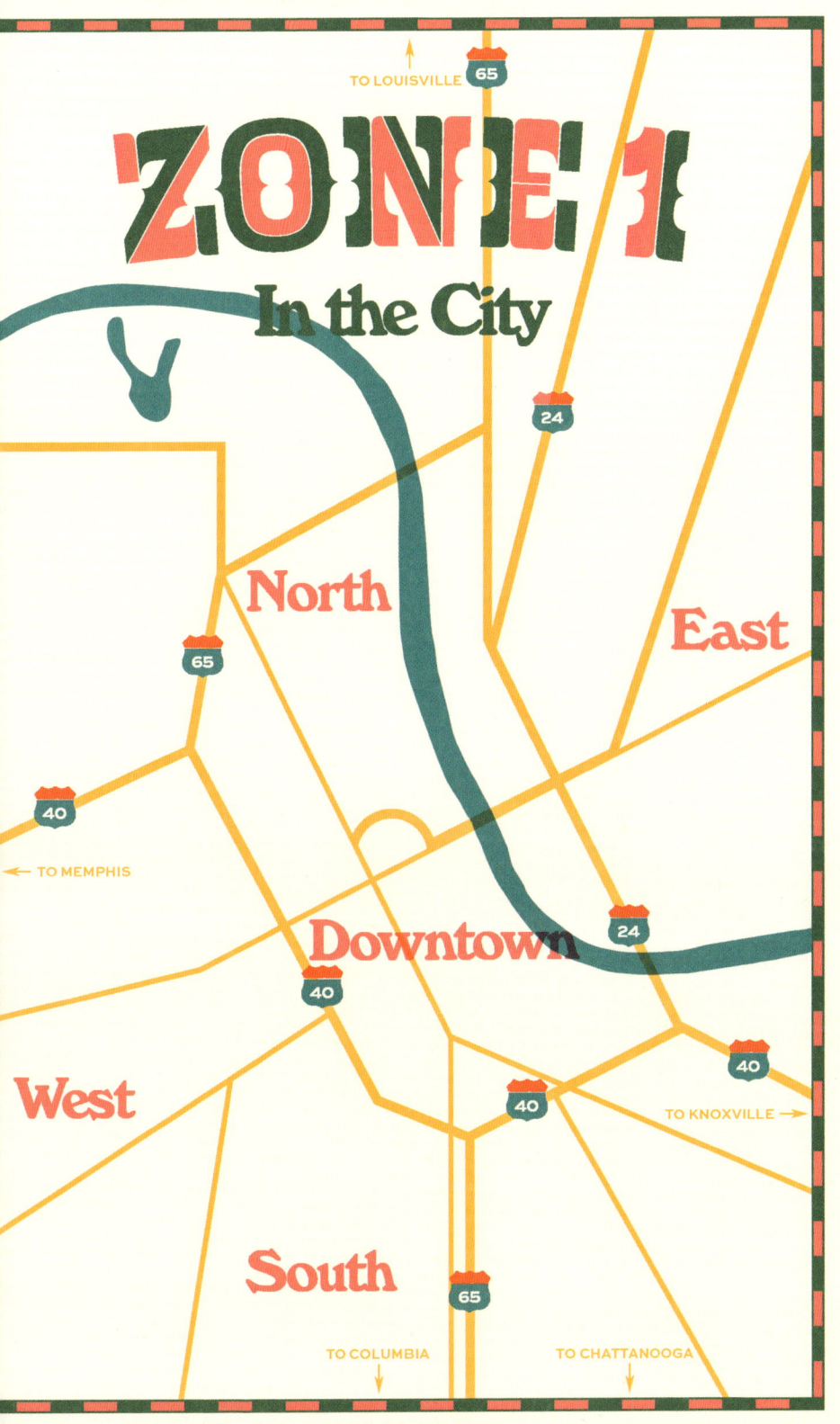

Downtown

Nashville's downtown district is a vibrant mix of honky-tonks, history, and heart. You can catch live music at every corner, from legendary spots such as the hallowed Ryman Auditorium to dive bars spilling with country tunes (and tourists). But there is so much more than that, from chill little jazz clubs to fancy fine art and museums with dancing patrons.

HONKY-TONK BADONKADONK

We owe this date to a rowdy riverboat captain. In 1885 one Thomas Green Ryman was apparently rolling in dough from his life of owning a thirty-five-ship fleet, running saloons, and engaging in various other scandalous behaviors. One night a very convincing revivalist preacher inspired Ryman to change his ways. Ryman ditched his shady activities and started fundraising to build a big church for all to hear the good word. Seven years after that he opened the doors to the massive new Union Gospel Tabernacle. Sometime later when he passed—now a well-respected member of the community (but possibly less fun)—the same convincing preacher proposed the Tabernacle's name be changed to the "**Ryman Auditorium**."

It began as a church but soon became hallowed grounds for music. In 1943 the already established Grand Ole Opry moved in to nest for the next thirty years. Patsy Cline, Elvis Presley, and Johnny Cash are but a few of the acts to play during the Opry years. (Speaking of dates, Johnny first met June Carter backstage here!) Those times may be over, but the Ryman's place in music history continues with an official Rock & Roll Landmark designation from the Rock & Roll Hall of Fame. Now everyone from Jenny Lewis to Wu-Tang Clan to Bob Dylan has played this room, and when you slide your hand into your date's back pocket and sway to the music, you'll feel it all. After you come out of the show, you should go ahead and commence bobbing and weaving through the tourists for a drink. For many years the Ryman didn't have any proper dressing rooms, which meant the world's most talented musicians would just hang around in the **alley in the back**, which is still the place to spot a star. And on more than one occasion, a headliner has been known to pop through the back alley right into **Tootsie's Orchid Lounge's** back door and keep the night going with an unofficial encore. Take in the historic Wall of Fame photos while tapping your feet to whoever is playing and remember personal space doesn't exist in a crowded bar.

One more stop before you leave the throngs in full NashVegas mode is **Robert's Western World**. This slightly sticky time capsule was once the home of the Sho-Bud Steel Guitar Company, founded by two legendary steel guitar players, Shot Jackson and Buddy Emmons. Nowadays it's a place where cowboy boots stack ceiling high and Pabst flows at early 2000s prices. In their nightly live music offerings, anyone and everyone has been known to make an appearance, all the way from Wynonna Judd to Lana Del Rey. If you've never been to a honky-tonk, this is a good one to wet your whistle at.

FOR THE RECORD

Many a memorable thing happened when we hit Y2K (other than our national concern that our computers would all simultaneously explode). Between episodes of a new show called *Survivor*, we'd pull out our squatty Nokia cell phones and begin the arduous multi-tap texting required to send a message to our friends about a new band we'd just seen with only two members—one of them a badass woman absolutely killing it on the drums. Now the White Stripes and their garage rock are well known, and front man Jack White co-owns a label, **Third Man Records**, with an attached shop. Pop in to see the black and gold western fringe shirts next to trinket dishes full of record pins or third (man) place ribbons. Take your date into the **Voice-O-Graph booth** to find a refurbished 1947 machine that can record up to two minutes of you singing sweet nothings to each other before pressing it onto a six-inch phonograph disc to commemorate your love for all time.

Take those squishy vibes over to the cozy den of **Rudy's Jazz Room**, swathed in red curtains and colorful Moroccan lamps. Both the menu and the vibe are New Orleans tinged, with smooth musicians playing while you suggestively raise your eyebrows at each other over cocktails. Jazz is experimental, and so is love, bayybee.

HOT TIP: If you have a super audiophile in your life, you can give them an extra surprise. Third Man's attached venue boasts the world's only live studio with direct-to-acetate recording capabilities. Finagle your way onto one of their tours of the inner workings of this process.

BE STILL MY ART

Nashvillians know how to brunch. It's a state of mind just as much as what's on your plate. One place that goes all in on the concept is **Adele's**. The legendary weekend brunch buffet inside their chic, sunny spot goes on for miles. Tiny cast-iron skillets with baked eggs, steamy hot buttermilk biscuits drenched in honey butter, attractive smoked salmon platters, and seasonal fruits piled high. Nothing says "I like you" like buying your crush an unlimited amount of cinnamon bread pudding.

Now off to the museum for a bit of culture, darling, and the **Frist Art Museum** does it right. The curatorial staff knows how to satisfy a diverse variety of interests with special exhibits ranging from the Dutch painting GOAT Rembrandt to fashion-forward projects with iconic pieces from legendary designer Alexander McQueen. Don your top hat, cane, and monocle (wait, that's just Mr. Peanut) for a trip to take it all in, or try one of the museum's fun **Drop-in Drawing** nights.

Keep an eye on their calendar for a **Frist Friday**, when highly attractive people who care about art convene for a night of music and partying and taking in the arts. A great place to come on a date for sure, but also not a bad place to go looking for one.

Now, we know the word *museum* can sound a lil' stuffy sometimes, but the **National Museum of African American Music's** tagline is "one nation under a groove." Wander through the chronologically arranged galleries while looking at giant wall mosaics of so many faces that changed the landscape of music (and many a make-out session, too, TBH). Billie Holiday, Boyz II Men, Lionel Richie, Janet Jackson, TLC, Prince, *Aretha*! The hits just keep coming. But the best part is seeing how happy the attendees are. Grandmas belting along to a Tina Turner video or college kids rapping every word to Run-DMC. When you get your parking validated, splurge on the five-dollar RFID wristband that allows you to create playlists of your favorite music as you go from their many interactive kiosks devoted to different genres.

Your playlists will be automatically emailed to you as soon as you leave, so you can head next door to the **Assembly Food Hall** for snacks and to compare notes. The hundred thousand-square-foot hall has something for every kind of mood with twenty restaurants, ten bars, one full-service restaurant, and a rooftop venue with music playing. No idea where to even begin? When in doubt, we say go to **Whisk Crêpes Café**, where Parisian-raised chef Julien Eelsen cooks perfectly crispy crêpes right in front of you, stuffed with all manner of delicious things, and given mouth-watering names, such as Brie My Baby or Madame Du-Berry.

More Fun

BOWL ME OVER Chic . . . bowling? Somehow it's possible at **Pinewood Social** where the cuties go to down craft cocktails while attempting to master the arduous 7–10 split on one of the reclaimed wooden lanes from a 1950s Bowl-O-Rama. There's also a pool! And Putt-Putt!

XOXO For a date unlike any other, try booking a session at **Lip Lab** to make your own signature custom shade of lipstick or balm. Not only will you create *the* perfect color, you also decide on a finish, from matte to high gloss, and add a little personal scent. You finish it off with an engraved case that reminds you of how cute this afternoon together was.

THE MAN IN BLACK Music lovers flock to see iconic guitars, vintage photos, and row upon row of glittering gold records at the **Johnny Cash Museum**. So much so that it's snagged the number one spot for music museums in the world by both *Forbes* and *National Geographic Traveler*.

SUCH GREAT HEIGHTS Get a stunning bird's-eye view of the city by hitting the daily happy hour at the glamorous **Harriet's Rooftop** bar. Sip on their reasonably priced house-made margarita with Shishito pepper–infused tequila, Ancho Reyes Verde, and clarified lime while feeling baller as hell.

North

In North Nashville there's no shortage of things to keep you and your date entertained. We'll cover Oktoberfest, the bountiful offerings of the farmers market, and activities to keep you busy on a weeknight (and make sure you have something to tackle together). Plus baseball and antiquing!

SWEET TREATS

If you've ever watched a rom-com with main characters wearing chunky sweaters and holding hands amid leaf-changing foliage, this one is for you. Step into the adorable micro-store **Taylor Street Art and Books** inside Gemantown's historic 100 Taylor Street Art Collective building. The owners proclaim themselves to be an "overcaffeinated artist" and a "nerdy ghostwriter," and they stock novels, art, and things like a deep dive into Tennessee's Bell Witch (which is a date we'll get to in a later chapter).

Assuming it's all going swimmingly, make the five-minute walk through Germantown to a dainty navy-painted brick house with a red door directing you to the goodness of **The Cupcake Collection**. Inside you'll find shelves stocked with the beloved sweet potato cupcake topped with freshly made cream cheese buttercream (as well as red velvet and carrot cupcakes). They even have pupcakes for Fido! Owner Mignon Francois famously started the company with the last five dollars to her name as a single mom and then parlayed that into a ten-million-dollar sugar empire.

ON THE MARKET

Let's be real. Sometimes on a date, we don't know what to talk about. Whether it's a first date and you're still trying to figure out common ground, or your millionth date when you just know everything about each other—every well runs dry occasionally. This is when a wander date comes in particularly handy because it means you continually have new stimuli in front of you, naturally bringing something to talk about.

Enter the stellar **Nashville Farmers' Market**, where the good stuff just keeps coming. There are the two large outdoor sheds with over one hundred bakers, cheese mongers, crafters, soap makers, jewelry designers, and folks slinging farm-fresh tomatoes. Check their website's seasonal produce list and you can form a recipe around it for the freshest dinner possible (together, obviously). There's also the twenty-seven thousand square-foot

Gardens of Babylon plant nursery with pretty little potted houseplants and multicolored coleus to stroll around.

When you tire of pointing at things and saying "cute!" pop into the **market's food court** with loads of restaurants serving everything from burritos to bibimbap. On the first Friday evening of each month, check out the on-site **Nashville Black Market** with more than forty Black-owned businesses selling wares and serving drinks. There's even dancing!

BRAT AUTUMN

Everyone has different versions of what role-playing is, but for this date, you're gonna need to go online and get lederhosen. Suppose you're not familiar with the sort of short-pants overalls with a distinctive stitching vibe. In which case: they are part of the traditional clothing of Bavaria along with the dirndl dress for women that, quite frankly, gives everyone a *smoking bod*. Or as better said by the folks at Lederhosens.com about the ensembles, they are "fun to wear and easy on the eye."

Once the said easy-on-the-eye clothing is secured, you two are heading to **Oktoberfest**. You'll find all the requisite fest things like "cheersing" beers the size of your head and downing various pickle-y or mustard-y things. You can't miss the main stage, where you might spot a fun dad band belting out polka renditions of Lady Gaga's *Bad Romance* or fire-breathing performers hypnotizing the crowd.

But the pièce de résistance is the annual pup parade, when folks bring their costumed pooches strutting their stuff. If your date doesn't swoon over seeing a corgi dressed as a bratwurst, a golden retriever in lederhosen, or a husky in a Superman cape, dump them immediately.

WEEK IN THE KNEES

We're all for a bop-around date, but on a weeknight, a one-stop shopping kind of vibe is the easiest way to sneak in some fun. And even better if they already have fun in the works. Like the waterfront taproom at **Monday Night Preservation Co.** inside a former factory with exposed brick and soaring ceilings, plus a whole lotta beer ranging from the lightest lagers to the darkest stouts. Check their weekly funtivity calendar for happenings such as Ballad Bingo—a bingo-meets-*Name-That-Tune* mashup for those with a musical ear—that's sure to ease any new daters into a comfortable teamwork state of mind.

The Skittles flavor of this same date takes place at **Frankie J's**, an LGBTQ+ bar with rainbow-colored rooms and furniture. On a group date, pop in for their weekly Monday night trivia quiz to win prizes and smug satisfaction. The crew here always have something going on, from *Drag Race* viewing parties to Broadway show tune singalongs to Ladies & Theydees night. Don't have a special someone figured out just yet? Head out into the big backyard and challenge a hottie to a game of cornhole, or better yet, make friends with the cutest dog. If you and the owner vibe, you might get to live with them both one day.

FOREPLAY

Group date alert! Not only is it far more cost effective on this particular adventure, it's way more fun to have the crew watch your **Topgolf** swings. This national chain is the size of an airplane hangar; open-air bays provide the perfect tee to smash golf balls out into a field of light-up targets. Your group gets its own bay (charged by rental time instead of by individual person), a server to keep beers and bites flowing, and a propane heater to keep it toasty even on a chilly day. It's kinda like bowling, but the ball goes a lot farther and you get to yell, "Who's your caddy?!"

First we're heading to the **Carl Van Vechten Gallery** at the historic **Fisk University**. Fisk, one of the nation's oldest historically Black colleges and universities, has more than 150 years of notable grads. Some of those impressive alumni include: world renowned poet Nikki Giovanni, W.E.B. Du Bois (one of the founders of the NAACP), and *Good Trouble* maker Congressman John Lewis.

The gallery, founded in 1949 and named for prominent writer/photographer Carl Van Vechten, quickly became a place to celebrate Black artists. Now you can pop into the little red-bricked gallery

and see rotating exhibits from prominent artists. And as long as we're talking Fisk-related dates, let's touch on the **Fisk Jubilee Singers**, who began singing in 1871, breaking racial barriers, raising money for their school, and eventually winning the 2008 National Medal of Arts—the nation's highest honor for artists. You can check their website for a future performance (and secure yourself a follow-up date).

And because appreciating history also means historic food, finish the date off with a stop at **Silver Sands Cafe**, who've been serving Nashville's iconic meat-and-three cafeteria-style dinner for more than seventy years with a different special every day of the week.

HOT TIP: If you want to read up on more local Black history, nearby bookstore **Alkebu-Lan Images** has a wide range of books and apparel from Black-owned businesses.

LET'S HAVE A BALL

Ah, America's pastime. No, not that. We're talking about baseball! But the beauty of the game is that it requires little to no effort or knowledge to appreciate watching someone swagger up to the plate and take a crack at bat. You get to hoot and holler from your seat as a collective group, and even for the total newbie, taking in a **Sounds game** at **First Horizon Park** makes for a pretty fun day. But going on a group date with the other ten thousand folks in the stadium can be daunting, so do a little preplanning to skip the stress and make the evening a home run (see what we did there?). Leave your bag at home or check the website for the strict rules about what you can bring in.

Then be sure to come in time to thoroughly enjoy all the field-sized games so you two can play before the team does. Shoot hoops on the life-sized Connect 4 game, show off your arm on the Speed Pitch throw, ping your pongs at table tennis, or play mini golf. Plus, boozy slushies and waffle fries!

RIDE 'EM COWBOY

Pick up your (reserved in advance) rides at **Green Fleet Bikes** because we're leisurely pedaling today. In mere minutes you'll cruise into the eleven-acre **Bicentennial Capitol Mall State Park**. There's loads to see, from the two-hundred-foot state map to the splashy fountains at the  shaped park.

But come fall, the trees of the main lawn turn brilliant shades of scarlet and orange, making it a particularly pleasant time for a visit. You can't leave without visiting the huge ninety-five-bell carillon perched on fifty large Greek-style columns. Each hour on the hour, the bells ring out the "Tennessee Waltz" for all to hear.

HOT TIP: If you prefer to let someone else do the guiding, Green Fleet Bikes has a popular Music City Bike Tour that'll take you around to all the sites, with a narrator along the way and selfie opportunities aplenty.

Now we're off again in search of a treat that shall be found at the bustling **Little Hats Italian Market**. Not only can you grab ice-cold Galvanina sodas or the prettiest little jars of giardiniera veggies from employees wearing tees with mustachioed mascot Cappy Cappelletti(!), but you can also refuel at their in-house deli. Superfans live for the eggplant parmesan sandwich with crispy cutlets on an Italian roll. Or there's *cacio e pepe* with freshly made linguini. Or crunchy then gooey fried arancini balls. Gah! Eat it all but remember to not get too stuffed since you still need to pedal back to the bike shop.

ANTIQUE ROAD SHOW

Pull up to your date's house and text, "Get in, we're going antiquing." But first up, no shopping-for-unnecessary-olden-things trip is complete without the requisite iced coffee. Stop by **Bloom & Brew Coffee** for a cup (and adding a snickerdoodle cookie to the tab never hurts) and then head to the Antique District on Goodlettsville's Main Street. There you can spend hours combing for treasure on just one street. There's the **Goodlettsville Antique Mall** with costume jewelry, floral trays, mid-century chairs, and ancient postcards. Down the way, at **Cast + Found Vintiques**, you'll find every lil' jar imaginable, brass candlesticks, and ornate bric-a-brac. **Rare Bird Antiques** is another massive mall, with ten thousand square feet of space filled with vendors offering Elvis and Metallica vinyl, sparkly geodes, and pretty milk glass pieces (not all in one display, of course). Hoo boy, that's a lot of stuff. Before leaving the neighborhood, you might need to stop into **Chef's Market Cafe & Takeaway**, where some cafeteria-style displays with Cajun salmon, mac and cheese, and greens are just waiting for you.

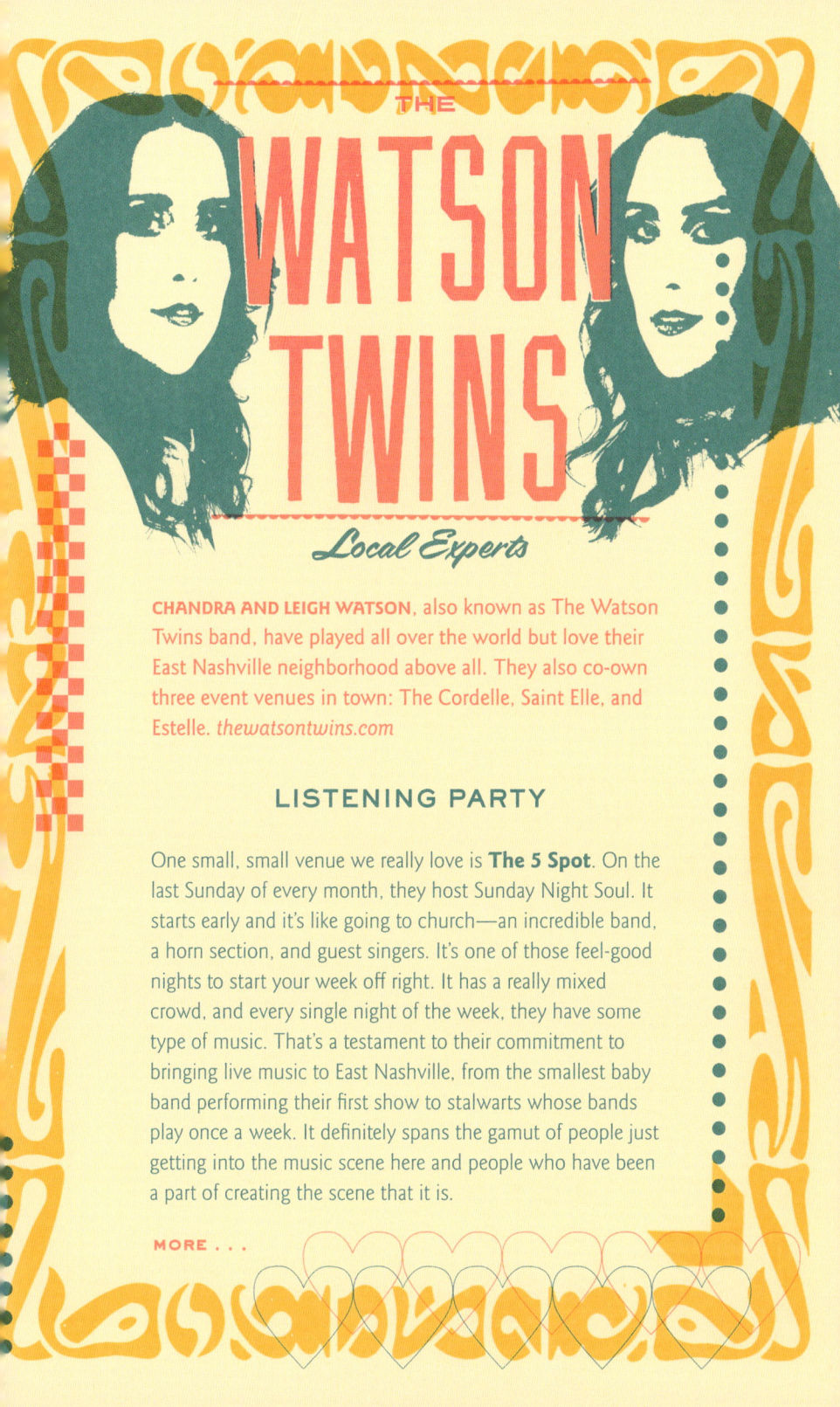

THE WATSON TWINS

Local Experts

CHANDRA AND LEIGH WATSON, also known as The Watson Twins band, have played all over the world but love their East Nashville neighborhood above all. They also co-own three event venues in town: The Cordelle, Saint Elle, and Estelle. *thewatsontwins.com*

LISTENING PARTY

One small, small venue we really love is **The 5 Spot**. On the last Sunday of every month, they host Sunday Night Soul. It starts early and it's like going to church—an incredible band, a horn section, and guest singers. It's one of those feel-good nights to start your week off right. It has a really mixed crowd, and every single night of the week, they have some type of music. That's a testament to their commitment to bringing live music to East Nashville, from the smallest baby band performing their first show to stalwarts whose bands play once a week. It definitely spans the gamut of people just getting into the music scene here and people who have been a part of creating the scene that it is.

MORE . . .

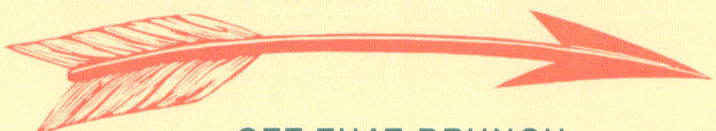

GET THAT BRUNCH

Julia Jaksic was the chef and collaborator with the folks from Jack's Wife Freda in New York, and she came down here to open her first restaurant, **Cafe Roze**. We had been to Jack's and loved that, so when we heard Julia was involved, we were so excited. She has such a unique palette and an incredible bar program with amazing cocktails such as beet martinis. Her Roze latte is infused with rose syrup—very signature to her and fantastic. The smoked trout toast is undeniable, and they're known for their french fries.

WHEN FRIENDS COME TO TOWN

One thing that's really fun, although you have to have buy-in from the people that are with you, is **The Nashville Palace**, which is a honky-tonk that isn't downtown. It's across from the Gaylord Opryland Resort, and they do line dancing and have a live band in front, and it's super sweet. They'll have a DJ and hype girls on the stage doing the dances—it's just people of all shapes, sizes, colors, everything. It's amazing. And it's just such a great energy to go there and dance with people you don't know, like a really quintessential Nashville experience because it's not downtown and it's a destination. We wrote a song about it called "The Palace."

TREAT HOPPING

First Saturday Art Crawl in Wedgewood-Houston is just south of downtown. It's spendy, so we do a snack at **Present Tense** and then go across the railroad tracks for a drink at **Never Never** bar,

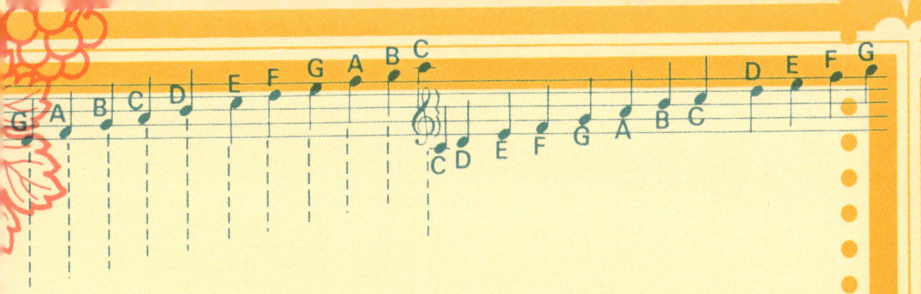

which is in the Arts District. All the galleries open up. Across the street from Never Never is **Bastion**, and the bar just does nachos. That's the only thing they serve: very delicious nachos. Videos play on the wall and they have cool seating. So that's fun—the whole arts area, a fancy appetizer, a drink, and then nachos for dessert.

A GROUP THANG

The hotel is called **Urban Cowboy**, but they have a bar on site called **Public House**. It has communal seating and, in the wintertime, firepits. **Roberta's** pizza truck is also there with a wood-fired oven, so you can just order a bunch of pizzas and sit, and people bring baby carriages and things like that. On Sunday nights they do jazz night in the **Parlour Bar**. That's the natural wine bar inside. So it's a nice place to gather people because there's something for everybody—whether the kids want pizza, or their parents want wine, or somebody needs a cocktail. We had our birthday there this year because people can just come and go, and they make amazing martinis there. It was perfect.

HUNTING & HOT SAUCE

GasLamp Antiques & Decorating Mall is really fun. It's an antique mall, but it has great weird jewelry finds, and it's got books, it's got furniture, it's got clothing, it's got jewelry, it's got all the artifacts. There are two GasLamp buildings there, and you wouldn't go there for any other reason than to go shopping. Except maybe for the really delicious taco spot there called **Baja Burrito**. So grab tacos and go to the antique store; that's definitely a move.

East

East Nashville is the city's cultural haven, known for its vibes and creative spirit. With murals on every corner, swaths of small businesses, and some killer coffee spots, it's a neighborhood that marches to its own beat. Add in pool days, long bike rides, and pizza nights, and you're going to like it here.

CLUB MED

Everyone knows a date becomes infinitely cooler if it has an element of surprise to it. Such is the case with the **Coral Club**, whose strip-mall/office-park building belies the cool within. Once through the nondescript door, you're met with a swanky other world. One with sculpted cement nooks and crannies, woven rattan lanterns, and masses of dripping, flickering candles. Snuggle into a corner with one of their house cocktails, such as the mezcal-forward Sunliner or an adorable dirty Tiny Tini.

Keep the Mediterranean vibes going across the street for dinner at **Peninsula**. If it's free, pull up to the stylish black-and-white star-tiled bar and give in to the unexpected. Founded by three veterans from Seattle's famed The Walrus and the Carpenter restaurant, the menu here is truly memorable. Funky things, such as a tempura sea foam butter endive or an actual cup of straight-up maitake mushroom broth, utterly delight alongside strains of Fleetwood Mac on the stereo. Don't forget about the signature gin and tonic menu.

DON'T PITA IN THE POOL

Lazy day dates aren't discussed enough. Sure it's great to go on a wild adventure, but have you ever heard of lounge life? For this chill get-together, start with brunch at **Butcher & Bee**. Inside, bunches of dried flowers hang from the ceiling and pothos winds around wooden booths.

At the honeycomb tile bar, spot a jaunty "Wu-Tang Forever" pennant flag hanging there. Opt for the adorable patio with monstera plants surely taller than your date. Whatever you do, be sure to set yourselves up for success by ordering

the whipped feta with hot honey and a fluffy-ass pita straight off a hot grill.
Even if the convo is lacking as you down caffeine to come alive, you'll be happy.

After all the carbs and coffee have been swallowed, mosey just down
the way to spend the day at the **Drift Hotel's pool**. The newish hotel offers
day passes to its outdoor pool, lounge chairs, cabanas, and changing rooms
through ResortPass.com. Snag a reservation then pack your trashy books, sunscreen, and maybe even a deck of cards to set up camp. Order cocktails from
the poolside service and let the games of Marco Polo commence!

JOYRIDE

Start your date by renting electric bikes at **Cornelia Fort Airpark**. Glide through the park's paved trail while you peruse the historical remnants of this once-bustling airport. Named after the first female pilot to die in war duty in the United States, and near where her family's farm once stood, a sign now pays homage with a quote from her: "I am grateful that my one talent, flying, was useful to my country." It was also known as *the* transport hub for the

Grand Ole Opry country stars, with famous names galore setting foot on these very runways. Patsy Cline, Lloyd "Cowboy" Copas, Hawkshaw Hawkins, and Randy Hughes were all en route to Cornelia Fort on March 5, 1963, when their tiny plane went down outside Camden, changing the industry overnight.

The city bought the airport in 2011, and now the abandoned runways are full of bike riders like yourself, couples holding leashes with happy pups, and kids with remote control cars. Zoom around to your heart's content before a short jaunt over to **Jeni's Splendid Ice Creams** (the Eastland Ave one) for a scoop of Cold Brew With Coconut Cream, which is just as delightful and invigorating as it sounds.

THE DATING GAME

P-I-Z-Z-A night! Kick it off at **Five Points Pizza**, a local gem known for its mouth-watering pies and relaxed vibe. Snag a table and begin a difficult deliberation. Whether you go for the artichoke-y goodness of the Super Bianca or the spicy Hot Hawaiian, each slice is a delicious mix of tangy ooey gooeyness. Share a pizza (or two) with a Greek salad while you get into the mental space for your post-dinner activities.

Take a short stroll over to **Up-Down Arcade Bar** to enter into a nostalgic haven filled with all the classic arcade games, pinball machines, and

Skee-Ball that you loved as a kid. Endorphins flood in to the *bam, bam, bam* beats from "Eye of the Tiger" as you two stride over to compare your *Pac-Man* prowess or go head-to-head shooting timed baskets. The combo of playful competition and witty banter means that, one way or another, someone's scoring big time.

SHOP HOP

Grab yer wallets and get in the car. First up? **Novelette Booksellers**. Among their thoughtfully curated shelves, you'll find an array of voices and stories. Whether you're drawn to instruction books on how to make witchy potions, captivating memoirs, or spicy romantasy novels, there's something here to spark conversation and inspiration. Pick up something you're both interested in and commence with an intimate book club for two.

Mere feet away, we dive into **Refinery Fragrances**, a luxury fragrance shop that promises an olfactory adventure. As you step inside, take in the exquisite scents from a number of niche perfume companies, such as Imaginary Authors, which packages innovative unique scents inside faux books. Take your time sampling different scents, with expert staff to guide you along your sensory journey.

One more to hit within this same brick building o' fun is the sweet little **Desert and Vine Botanical Supply**. Flourishing shelves hold all your houseplant dreams. There are little pink peperomias and elegantly striped tradescantias, beanies embroidered with "Plant Daddy," and disco-ball plant hangers to outfit your entire space.

Celebrate your hauls (and maybe spend a little more money) with a pop into **Vinyl Tap**, where you can unwind with a drink and get lost in their piles of vinyl records. This unique spot combines a bar with a record shop, creating a relaxed atmosphere perfect for browsing and discovering new music. Sip on the "Wake Me Up Before You Go-Go" signature cocktail with coconut rum, espresso liquor, cold brew, and Oaxacan bitters to flip those records double time. We recommend you each pick up an album that soundtracked your life in some way and then tradesies for a few days so you get to know each other a smidge deeper.

BYE-BYE, BIRDIE

Nashville is a chosen city for many reasons. And for the largest swallow in North America, the Purple Martin, it's a pit stop before they make their winter trek to South America. Late summer these little birdies—that appear to have a glamorous purple feather cape RuPaul would surely approve of—swirl in the sky at dusk by the thousands. In 2020 they snagged headlines when 150,000 of the birds roosted next to the Symphony Schermerhorn Center. It's something to be seen with a special person who celebrates bird phenomena as much as you. And if you like it and have an open area in your yard, consider installing a Purple Martin gourd housing system to give these little cuties one more option to spend the night on their long journey.

GROUPIES

Let's hear it for the group date. It's low presh for all involved, and you get to spend time with your cutie and your friends all at once. Bonus points if it's affordable. For this one steer the posse to the adorable yellow house that is **Rosemary & Beauty Queen**, nestled in the Five Points neighborhood, and walk through to the equally adorable deck and backyard sitch. With a strictly enforced seven-to-ten-person party limit, you can reserve a private rooftop cabana to nosh on simple sammies and sip giggle-inducing THC-laden cocktails or refreshing ginger mocktails.

Once you've savored every last drop, it's time to take the party up a notch at **The Lipstick Lounge**. One of the few lesbian bars left in the country (in the 1980s there were six times as many), this all-are-welcome venue is perfect for a night of camaraderie and fun. In 2024 it even received the first rainbow crosswalk in the city, unveiled right outside its doors. Head straight forward to the karaoke stage, where your group can cheer each other on as you belt out your favorite tunes. When in doubt, start with "9 to 5" to begin a singalong that will engage every possible age demographic. That's the power of Dolly.

OPRY OPRY, READ ALL ABOUT IT

Full disclosure on this date: we are going full kitsch. If you have a sort of elegant minimalism type of vibe and don't like silliness or things being highly extra, this might not be for you. This preamble may have clued you in to the fact that we're about to wax poetic on all things Opryland. We're also sort of breaking our own rules about the zones because while this spot may only be a scant twenty minutes from downtown Nashville, and you easily could visit it for a couple of hours, we envision a world where you have enough time for a full-blown staycation. This allows you to engage with the bountiful sensory overload options, starting with jungle wonder at **Gaylord Opryland Resort & Convention Center**.

Okay, so maybe you've at least heard whisperings of this famed tourism hot spot, but here's the quickie version. Opened in 1977, the hotel was built to support the Grand Ole Opry (which we're gonna get to) and was next to the long-gone Opryland USA amusement park (RIP). Starting in the 1980s, they began adding more rooms and plant-filled atriums, culminating in the glorious

4.5-acre Delta Atrium, which is so massive that it has its own river complete with a boat ride. It's free for the public to come walk around and take it all in, and it has a small village of restaurants. If this live-tropical-garden-meets-convention-center description isn't enough to tell you there's an unusual juxtaposition of demographics here, I don't know how else to clue you in.

Eat a soft pretzel the size of your head among the perky bromeliads and long palms stretching to the glass ceiling. Watch the little boat filled with grandpas excitedly looking at a faux alligator on the moss green water and enjoy the frivolous wonder of it all. Don't linger too long, though; shows at the **Grand Ole Opry** start at seven p.m.

HOT TIP: At Christmas this place starts looking like it's straight out of a Charles Dickens novel. The outside and gardens sparkle with millions of lights, carolers in costumes sing, ice sculptures are displayed, fantastic ice skaters perform, and gleeful snow tubing takes place. It's enough to make Santa look boring.

A hundred years ago, the *Grand Ole Opry* radio show started as the *WSM Barn Dance* in the fifth-floor radio studio of the National Life and Accident Insurance Company building downtown. It's safe to say it's the most fun thing to ever come out of an insurance building. Over the years it's been at the Belcourt Theater and the Ryman Auditorium before setting up camp at this spot in the '70s. If you think of any great country artist, they've performed at the Opry: Roy Acuff, Loretta Lynn, Hank Williams, Johnny Cash, Vince Gill, Garth Brooks, Emmylou Harris, Carrie Underwood. The list goes on and on.

Its impact can't be overstated and if you want to really dive in, do so with legendary documentarian Ken Burns's *Country Music*. He manages to drill down decades of music history into eight two-hour episodes, but it was only possible with the help of the Opry's archive team. They were the largest contributor of photographs to the miniseries, supplying more than 211 images, plus 30 video clips.

Go watch one of these fabled live shows arm in arm by hopping onto the hotel's free shuttle to the venue. Tickets can reach the fiftyish dollar range for nosebleeds (which still sound great, BTW) and up to $$$$ for full VIP backstage experiences with all the bells and whistles. That includes a private backstage tour before the show, an in-person howdy from one of the night's performers, access to the premium lounge with fancy cocktails and snacks, plus sitting *on stage* for the first half of the show. It's a pretty penny, for sure, but a night to remember for a milestone event celebration.

The next morning we're going to up the childish antics to a new level by hitting the resort's water park, **SoundWaves**. Yes, we're encouraging a full waterslide date. Note that the park says the only way you can get in is by booking an overnight SoundWaves package, so that's one more reason for #staycationlife. Shoot down the Bass Drop—a high-speed, open-flume body ride that drops you six stories in a total free fall! Laugh maniacally while you attempt to surf on the fake waves or hold hands while you float the lazy river,

complete with LED lights and tunes! Make sure to seek out the Diamond Pool
when the joyful screeching gets too loud. Blessedly, it's an adults-only spot.

Before you head home, stroll over to America's forgotten obsession, *the mall*.
Remember how much fun malls were? **Opry Mills** still is. Drop some coin on
new kicks. Give a thumbs-up to any goth teens lingering outside Hot Topic. Hit
the massive IMAX theater to watch a dumb action movie for no other reason
than "spending time together is nice." But if you're doing this mall *correctly*, you
will, in fact, get a meal at the **Rainforest Cafe**. Once a decorative-jungle-with-
weird-animatronics staple nationwide, as malls have dwindled, so too have our
beloved Rainforest Cafes. This one here is not only the sole one in Tennessee,
it's one of less than twenty left in the country. So down that Anaconda Pasta,
which likely doesn't have real anacondas in it, and finish it off with the Sparkling
Volcano brownie. This is a conservation effort, people.

More Fun

A CASE OF THE MONDAYS Put on your finest vintage gear and get your booties down to **The 5 Spot**. Every week, it's **Motown Monday**, where you can boogie down to all the greats from Smokey to the Supremes.

A ROZE BY ANY OTHER NAME Cafe Roze is officially adorable every day of the week, with food as pretty as it is delicious, but try snagging a reservation during one of their special jazz nights for something extra sexy.

FRIDAY I'M IN LOVE Have a standing First Friday night date with your love all summer long on the spacious outdoor patio at your favorite Aussie café, **Hearts**, where they screen a flick while you munch on a pastry.

DEEP DIVE If you like dive bars, Dolly Parton decor, and Velveeta cheese, then you must pay a visit to East Nashville's oldest dive, **Dino's**. Hey, even Anthony Bourdain wanted these burgers.

South

We love a neighborhood with variety, and the southern chunk of Nashville offers that in abundance. Cheering at soccer games, scouring flea markets, racing the clock of an escape room, looking for stars, seeing a clouded leopard, and so much more. Get those calendar apps open; you have places to go.

FOOTLOOSE & FANCY FLEA

Some dates do not call for high romance. The second date, where you think you like each other but are still feeling it out. The ones with your BFF instead of SO. Or the one where money is a little tight. We got you.

Grab a little drink treat at the rainbow-walled **Matryoshka Coffee** shop. It's a teeny little happy nook of a spot to catch up with each other. Not only is the place as cute as the Russian nesting dolls it's named after, but the coffee has flair, too. Try the Gas Station Capp—a take on a vanilla cappuccino with brown sugar, cardamom, nutmeg, and a sprinkle of edible glitter.

Then get thy caffeinated buns over to the **Nashville Flea Market** at the fairgrounds. Founded in 1969, this once-a-month wonder gives visitors the goods with more than 300 vendors from thirty states. They even claim to be one of the top ten flea

markets in the country (take that, Arkansas!). And that sure seems to check out as you wander aisle after aisle with every seeming retail category in the universe represented. There are vintage denims, western shirts with fringe aplenty, boots on boots on boots, vintage Polaroid cameras, ancient-looking Coca-Cola signs, Depression glass in every color, vintage badminton sets, and enough multicolored crocheted afghans to outfit an entire neighborhood. And, baby, that's just the tip of the iceberg. Get lost here together as long as you like.

CAN I KICK IT?

You know what's freaking fun? Chanting. Also scream-singing with thirty thousand of your closest friends. Also shouting "GOALLLLLLLLLL" at the top of your lungs. You can do all this and see world-class soccer players in action at **Geodis Park**. It's not only the largest soccer-specific stadium in the country but the largest in all of North America! A literal BFD.

Don't know a thing about soccer? Get hyped for your upcoming tix with frequent cuddle-watch parties of *Ted Lasso* or *Welcome to Wrexham*, where a bit of soccer education comes through evenly matched with a lot of heartwarming hotties of all kinds. Day of, take in the parade of Nashville SC superfans (*hooligan* is a controversial word), who are hyping up the crowd and waving ginormous team flags before the show begins. Grab a soda, start cheering, and occasionally yell, "Was he offside?!" to look in the know.

Afterward, either celebrate the win or soothe your sorrows in the bar half of nearby **Bastion**. Here you can clink a drink and then dive into their celebrated tinfoil trays of nachos piled high with all the fixin's.

GET OUT

The challenge of working together against the clock in an escape room might be equivalent to six months of couples therapy. So . . . perfect date! The mysteries that need solving at **The Escape Game (Berry Hill)** have earned it heaps and heaps of praise. Normally the internet can't even agree on whether the toilet paper gets loaded under for the pull method or over for hit and spin, but somehow over ten thousand folks have given this place a five-star review. It's an online miracle.

Here you can eschew some of the common super-violent escape room themes (a real romance buzzkill). Ones to try include The Depths, involving rumblings of strange experiments from an undersea laboratory that has come to light. You'll need to go into the depths of the ocean to get to the bottom of it. Another fan favorite is Ruins: Forbidden Treasure. Here your Indiana Jones-esque adventure begins on an old plane wreck near the legendary Ehlari Ruins. And, of course, there's mythical treasure you need to go after with only your wits to help you.

Now, they have games that run into the witching hour if you want to get into that kind of mindset. But there's also nothing that stops you from solving mysteries right after brunch. If that's more your lane, hit up **The Nashville Jam Co.** before you go. The little house-turned-café serves and sells all manner of delicious local jams—from peach-habanero to apple-bourbon to perfect blackberry—to their jam fanatics (jamatics?). But they also gifted the world a twist on a breakfast burrito that includes fried green tomatoes and pimento cheese. Brilliant.

WOO-WOO
YOUR LOVER

When you're ready to chillax in a way you've likely never tried before, boy, have we got an idea for you. The **Spa Haus's** Seven Senses Crystal Energy Healing Bed. Imagine in your mind's eye, if you will, a crystal bed with chakra lights positioned above you, the hertz frequency level of your choice, binaural beats coming through your noise-canceling headphones, and a vibrating Biomat below you made of heated amethyst gems. It is the vibiest of vibes with even more things we don't fully understand, such as pulsing electromagnetic fields and gamma waves, but maybe it'll be a cure for what ails ya!

You've just done all the good work to your bod, might as well keep the wellness going just a few feet away at **Vui's Juice Cafe**. Down delicious smoothies such as their Tropical Blue number with Blue Majik spirulina, mango, pineapple, ginger, lemon, and juiced apple. Or try the Açaí Bowl topped with local Nashville honey, cacao nibs, and crunchy granola. Hungrier than that? There's also the regular **Vui's Kitchen** right there with picnic tables and cornhole. Plus banh mis with meat or veggie options that all come on perfectly charred grilled bread with a soft outer bit and crispy inner bit and topped with a drippy pickled slaw.

A BOY NAMED ZOO

Fun fact. Or not so fun fact, really. If you're an animal lover, some zoos are beyond depressing, which is not ideal for dating life. But let's talk about the **Nashville Zoo at Grassmere** and the Association of Zoos and Aquariums (AZA) for a moment. The AZA is an independent accrediting organization that only gives a thumbs-up to institutions with the utmost standards for animal care and welfare. In fact only 10 percent of the 2,800 wildlife exhibitors licensed by the Department of Agriculture get an official pat on the head. And Nashville Zoo is one of them thanks to their conservation research, habitat protection, public education, and breeding programs for endangered animals such as the majestic clouded leopard. More than thirty-five clouded leopard cubs have been born at the zoo since 2009, ensuring some of the best cute kitten sighting opportunities in the country.

HOT TIP: You're already likely going to need to hit the restroom after a day of perusing the zoo, but make sure you do so with adorable tamarin monkeys bouncing by in the floor-to-ceiling windows as you wash your hands.

Okay, so now that we know you can walk through the doors feeling good, let's deliver more cool news. Each holiday season **Zoolumination** becomes the largest Chinese lantern festival in the country with more than one thousand silk lanterns sculpted into glorious magic across three miles of pathways. Stroll hand in hand through the multicolored Animal Trail, where you'll encounter mythical beasts such as winged tigers, an outer-space field, a Chinese village (including a lantern of a man doing the famed Lion Dance), a giant dragon you can walk through, and even a North Pole village. Because that's where Santa lives!

STARS, THEY'RE JUST LIKE US

Leave it to the geniuses at **Vanderbilt Dyer Observatory** to thoughtfully plan the timing of their "Bluebird on the Mountain" and "Opera on the Mountain" concert series to coincide with the brilliant color explosion of sunset. Picture this: You pack a picnic dinner for your cutie and chitchat as the sun goes down and the stars come up. Music starts to play as you smile at each other and hold hands across your blanket, realizing you are the main characters in your own rom-com. As if that's not enough, after the series, you go to the observatory's fancy Seyfert and DeWitt Telescopes to see the stars and planets up in the sky shining down on your love. Yeah, it is all as cute as it sounds.

READING IS FUN-DAMENTAL

Mini book club alert! Before you launch this lake date, you've got to get on the same page by reading the same book. And we're not snobs when it comes to what—graphic novels, poetry collections, celebrity memoirs, smutty audiobooks—they all count. But agree to consume the same thing and then set out for **Radnor Lake State Park**.

Enjoy the scenic drive past stately homes with sprawling lawns large enough to easily host thirty simultaneous games of *Twister* (now *that's* a date idea!) while you compare notes on your book of choice. Once you arrive at the 1,400-acre park with a large lake smack in the middle, pop onto one of the easy

PARNASSUS

BOOKS

NASHVILLE

(and ADA-accessible) walks, the Spillway Trail, and keep on with the character arc chat. The mulched trail starts behind the Walter Criley Visitor Center and heads up to the lake, with several observation spots to stop and take in the rushing water sounds from the creek and the hooded and Kentucky warblers proudly singing in what all sounds like a white-noise app on the rainforest setting. You can extend the afternoon by popping onto the Lake Trail to turn this mini jaunt into a proper walk. Keep an eye out for gorgeous bright-red scarlet tanagers peeping out of the greenery.

When you're all talked out and your limbs feel loose, make one more stop at **Parnassus Books**. Owned by lauded author Ann Patchett, who once made *Time Magazine's* 100 Most Influential People in the World(!) list. Patchett opened this little jewel after noticing that the big box stores had run all the independently opened bookshops out of town. That's an ethos we like, so spend freely on other Nashville authors (such as *Beverly Hills, 90210* star Jason Priestley's highly entertaining memoir!) and make sure to snag your next co-read for your mini book club so you can do this one all over again.

FIESTA FOREVER

Head to **Plaza Mariachi's** pop-up weekend flea market in the parking lot. There's the typical flea market stuff, but you can stop at the produce booths for a variety of vibrant, tropical fruits that promise a sweet taste of adventure. Pick out some juicy mangoes, ripe papayas, and perhaps a few fun treats that you've never tried before from friendly vendors. Head inside Plaza Mariachi, where the indoor mall with outdoor decor seems familiar to anyone who's ever paid a visit to Las Vegas. Amble through the little eclectic shops with names such as **Diva's Fashion #1**, marveling at glittery sequin dresses perfect for stage outfits, quinceañeras, or anyone who loves a bit of sparkle. Explore fun candy shops and maybe even spot a cheeky, not-so-official Louis Vuitton ensemble.

After shopping, head to the food court for a delicious authentic meal with options from Peru to Mexico to Honduras. Note the entertainment calendar before you go and time your meal with one of the shows, be it a live mariachi band performing on stage in full regalia, a traditional family *Lotería* game night, or colorful folk dancers. Don't stop with the good vibes. On your drive home, turn the dial to a Pedro Infante playlist—the hottest singer/movie star in Mexico in the 1950s. His romantic ranchera tunes and velvety voice will transport you to another era, adding a touch of timeless romance to your journey home (and that goodnight kiss).

BIG DISC ENERGY

For today's date we're headed to the **Cane Ridge Disc Golf** course to swap out the traditional golf club for the more avant-garde frisbee. If you've never played disc golf before, let's get you up to speed on the easy breezy rules. The goal is to have the least throws to get your frisbees into the baskets for each hole. One stroke is counted each time your disc is thrown. And the player with the least strokes on the previous hole is the first to tee off on the next hole. That's enough to get you started.

Now that you have the rules, we'll get to work on some kind of joke about scoring, and you just enjoy lining up in the alleyway of trees, blissful shade covering you in the hottest months, while you square your shoulders, twist, and fling your frisbee into the ether. There are two courses: one for pros that will give you a run for your money and one for the total newbies. Like regular golf, it's just an excuse to hang out together outside, and that's the real win. Make a batch of fruit tea before you go and clink your thermoses to a successful game.

West

West Nashville is a dreamy blend of outdoor adventure and lively fun. Sip a sunny drink next to lounging turtles, wander in a dreamy garden for hours, enjoy the myriad of dates available at Centennial Park, hang with drag queens in the morning, and embrace the importance of a leisurely solo date.

MANUAL STIMULATION

Is there anything better than taking yourself out for a leisurely solo date after a long week? Better yet, one stuffed with rejuvenating culture, carbs, and entertainment to thoroughly rev you up? This one takes place in the sweet little Hillsboro Village and commences at the ye olde **Pancake Pantry**—a local fave for over sixty years.

Did you know that archeologists researching the Shanidar Cave complex in Iraq recently discovered evidence of the world's oldest cooked meal by the Neanderthals? Any idea what it was? You guessed it. Turns out that, seventy thousand years ago, our ancient ancestors were also making pancakes. So when you tuck into that pillowy Smoky Mountain Buckwheat stack or the precious seasonal Pineapple Upside Down Cake, know the urge is a primal one deep in our DNA. Savor each bite as you leisurely do all the things on your phone—Wordle, crosswords, carefully internet-stalking a crush while making sure to not accidentally like a photo deep in their feed—until you're ready for a walk.

Now's the time for some great window shopping, from pink-painted brick-and-mortars to a swap meet pop-up in a gas station parking lot. Enjoy a wander and some time to yourself. Then keep it going by taking in a matinee at the **Belcourt Theater**.

HOT TIP: Once a year, keep an eye out for the awwwww-inducing montage reel of the internet's best cat videos with ticket sales going to benefit local cat rescues around the country.

Originally built in 1925 as a silent movie house with the biggest stage in town, the nonprofit theater is now devoted to helping audiences understand the importance of film. That means Q&As with filmmakers, panel conversations with experts, their signature Queer Qlassics programming, and even a High School Film Club. But don't you worry, it's also a place where you can slide on in for a midday matinee, get a soda the size of your head, and take in a flick.

Before you leave the neighborhood, take a cue from Miley Cyrus and stop at the color-bursting **A Village of Flowers** to buy a bouquet for yourself to take home. You deserve it.

OLD-FASHIONED FUN

How to tackle the age-old dilemma: consume carbs or climb a faux wall? The only solution is, of course, to do both. First pay a visit to **Hero Doughnuts & Buns**, and the race to see who says, "I'd like to order *your* hot buns" first is on. At the little doughnut chain with a handful of locations across the south, folks go nuts for the melt-in-your-mouth sweetness of the Boston Cream Filled, but we implore you to give the Maple Sea Salt and cup of coffee combo a go.

Once you're properly buzzing on sugar and caffeine, work out those twitchy muscles by scampering up a series of confettied, colored jugs protruding from the walls at **Climb Nashville West**. Snag two reasonably priced day passes to try a new activity together. The fee will get you a gym tour, an orientation, an auto belay lesson, and a top rope belay lesson (those words will make sense after the lessons). Then put your trust and teamwork to the test by climbing up their sky-high indoor wall. It's as far a cry from a dating rut as can be.

ALL DOLLED UP

Drag queens and brunch go together like mob wives and leopard print. And **Suzy Wong's Drag'n Brunch** knows how to do both (and maybe all of it, but they aren't no snitches). The name is an ode to the 1960 film *The World of Suzie Wong*. And the menu is an ode to, well, breakfast. Start off each of the weekend shows with a basket of beignets and fruit, then say hello to three queens with elegant names like Blush, Deception, or Vanity—who flip, twirl, and sashay down the runway. This is truly the cure for seasonal depression.

Keep the self-care going at nearby **Shira's Nail Bar**, where a whole team of nail artists awaits at the press of an online scheduling button. Zone out in the chair and try the Rocket Spa Pedicure with all the bells and whistles. The massage chair rolls your buns around while your feet soak. Then come the necessary callus removal, sweet honey sugar scrubs, a toasty hot stone massage, and a regular lotion foot massage—all topped off with the perfect pop of color. Look, if you're gonna get into the Feet Pics lifestyle, you gotta start looking fresh.

Flower Power

Begin your date with a romantic walk at **Magnolia Lawn** near Vanderbilt University. The sight of the magnificent magnolia trees in full bloom sets a captivating fairytale-like scene with creamy, dinner plate–sized flowers perfuming the air. Stroll hand in hand and do your best to talk about things besides work. Keep that lovely step-in-step going another ten minutes for the antithesis of a nature walk with a visit to **Old Glory**.

The hidden gem of a bar is nestled inside the former boiler room of White Way Cleaners. That makes for a unique industrial setting, with its sixty-foot-tall ceilings, a behemoth original chimney stack surrounded by swinging plant vines, and a grand curved staircase. Grab a cocktail and make your way to the cozy upstairs nook, where you can soak in the ambiance of this distinctive vibe and each other. Awwwww.

PARKS AND REC

New York has Central Park. San Francisco has Golden Gate Park. And Nashville has **Centennial Park**. Each one is packed with frolicking kids, couples gazing eye to eye, and someone still going for it with a hacky sack. This 132-acre wonder has had many lives—an eighteenth-century farm, the state fairgrounds, and an eleven-year stint as a racetrack. In 1897 it was the site of the Tennessee Centennial Exposition, which prompted the building of the Parthenon replica and a movement toward making it a long-lasting park. Now it features Watauga Lake, walking trails, a dog park, a sunken garden bed, the Centennial Art Center, and so much more, making the date options plentiful.

Get Them to the Greek

The Greek word *eudaimonia* loosely translates as a combination of well-being, happiness, and flourishing. And flourishing ye shall be when you stop into **Taziki's Mediterranean Cafe** for orders of their spicy harissa hummus and tangy tzatziki sauce loaded up on gyros or overflowing rice bowls. Take all that goodness to go as you meander across the park to the **Parthenon**.

Stretch out on a patch of grass and munch your goods while talking history facts for a moment. Nashville is approximately five thousand miles from Athens, but looking at this architectural wonder, you wouldn't know it. This Tennessee Parthenon is an exact full-scale replica, down to the forty-two-foot Athena statue on display, just as it was in ancient Greece. Go inside the museum to soak in the Greek history as well as the surprising collection of lovely landscape paintings from nineteenth- and twentieth-century American artists. Beyond the permanent collection, there's always an interesting rotating exhibit, so check the website before you go. Assuming the magical combo of feta, art appreciation, and intellectualism went well, we recommend wrapping the night up with a special toga party for two. Wink, wink.

Kids Incorporated

The entire point of a date is that you're telling another person that you value spending time with them. And while that's most often a romantic partner, it can be friends, family, and yes, kiddos, too. So be the rad parent/cool uncle/hip godmother and ask a little one if they'll go on a special hang time with you. The first way to their hearts? A visit to **Elliston Place Soda Shop**, which has been keeping locals sugared up since 1939.

Sit at the counter and make a permanent memory together by splitting the classic banana split. That's scoops of chocolate, vanilla, and strawberry loaded up with a host of toppings, and finished off with a split banana, whipped cream, and the requisite cherry on top. Perfection.

After that, it's a visit to the **Storybook Walk** in Centennial Park. As you meander along the path around Watauga Lake, stop at each book placard and read a different page of the story you take in together as you go. Every month is a new book, so you can make this a regular twosome activity. It's also a good time to talk nature with a wave to the paddling ducks and a peek across the water to the central island. There, away from people, is a collection of beehives so that the bees can do their jobs of pollinating flowers and trees around the park. You can even buy honey from the Centennial Park bees (well, made by them, not actually buy it from the bees, though that would be cute) in the **Parthenon Museum Store**. Science is cool!

Tune Town

A cheap date doesn't have to be a bad thing. And it isn't when it comes to the **Musicians Corner** series at the park. Since 2010 the **Centennial Park concert series**—a month-long string of free concerts—has taken place in the spring and again in the fall. This means that the grassy stage has seen everyone from Emmylou Harris to the Blind Boys of Alabama to the Watson Twins. Local vendors set up booths selling boba tea and aggressively large corn dogs, as well as candles and doodads that are worth a look. Then it's about laying out a blanket and cuddling with your cutie while the band plays—the best bang for your buck of all.

A BIT CHEEKY

If you haven't noticed our subtle garden propaganda by now, we might as well come right out and admit it. We are strongly pro garden dates. Winding along manicured paths while holding hands. Phones being ignored in pockets or even, gasp, *left in the car*. Stopping to literally smell the roses while smiling at each other. Every single thing about it promotes quality time and simple pleasures.

And if we're gonna talk about a good garden date in Nashville, we *must* talk about **Cheekwood Estate & Gardens**. You've likely heard bits about the history of the place. How the elder Cheeks got into the wholesale grocery game, then the coffee game, and then a Maxwell House "good to the last drop" coffee empire that eventually netted the family an animated GIF of money raining. That kind of money meant the family went "full mansion with elegant gardens," moving into the manor on Thanksgiving 1932.

But all the facts aside, have you thought about the truly baller parties they must've hosted here? Including one memorable summer fete in 1933 that transformed the lawn into the Acropolis, where guests were assigned either a Greek or Roman god/goddess and expected to arrive in costume. Mark Zuckerberg could never!

Now the fancy place is a fifty-five-acre botanical garden and estate open to the public for all kinds of lovely strolling. There's absolute childish glee to be found with model trains running in and out of trees and dioramas in the **Turner Seasons Garden**. There are turtle-filled ponds in the stately **Blevins Japanese Garden**. There are reasons to fall in love with gardeners who go ride-or-die for each other in the wildflower haven of the **Howe Garden**.

Go for the day and see it all. Grab a simple lunch from the on-site **Café 29** and take it to go, settling into one of the many picturesque spots for a meal, such as the benches by the stream in front of the manor or near singing frogs in the **Robinson Family Water Garden**. If you come in a mood to lollygag, you can't go wrong.

HOT TIP: It's a great visit year-round, but be sure to note their calendar for seasonal indulgences, such as an explosion of 250 thousand spring flower bulbs, a summer concert series under the stars, or a one-mile holiday light extravaganza.

While you're still in the mood to appreciate the elegance of days gone by, you might as well seal the deal with a trip to **Sperry's Restaurant** for a happy hour cocktail. Move past the stained-glass windows into a dark den of aged wood with a host of regular clientele who've clearly been coming since the place opened in 1974. Sit at the beautiful bar for a perfectly shaken dirty martini and toast your successful garden day. If you really want to impress your date, you can casually toss out this fun nugget: the salad bar here was the first one in Nashville. Innovation!

MOON RIVER

This one won't look like much from the parking lot, but walk down the gangplank and out to the adorable patio of the **Blue Moon Waterfront Grille**. Grab a waterfront table, order some signature tacos, and start ogling the recently developed view around you. Canadian geese, sometimes with their goofy babies, swim in circles. Turtles poke up their little heads and a mallard showing off his skiing skills whizzes by. All of this while an eclectic soundtrack, ranging from Harry Belafonte's "Day-O" to Devo's "Whip It," plays.

Sitting next to your honey with the sun smiling down while you watch folks in boats tootle by, prepping their rods to catch striper and bass, is perfectly lovely in itself. But let's say you visit **Boat Rental Nashville** located in the same marina. Here you can rent pontoon boats big enough for your whole crew and set out on the Cumberland River for the day. Try renting the Aloha Tropical, which comes *with a slide*, a sound system, cushy seats, and a lily pad to toss out onto the water for swimming times. You can still hit up Blue Moon for some food and fun, but now you have the option to cruise right up to it.

More Fun

ON WITH THE SHOW

At **Exit/In**, the vibe is electric during a show. This iconic spot has been a cornerstone of Nashville's music scene since 1971. The venue's memorabilia-covered walls pay homage to decades of music history in a way that makes you feel the ghosts of past performances reverberating through the air.

ANIMAL COLLECTIVE

Head to the **Cross-Eyed Critters Watering Hole** karaoke bar at the Graduate Hotel for a night of unforgettable fun. With its quirky animatronic band and lively atmosphere, it's an almost terrifying twist on the classic karaoke experience. Belt out your favorite tunes with friends and wonder why Chuck E. Cheese never let you sing at parties.

FASHIONABLY LATE

Discover **The Late Great**, a hidden gem with a classic speakeasy vibe. Tucked in the heart of Music Row you'll find plush crushed red velvet couches, sexy cocktails, and dim, inviting lighting.

JAR JAR DRINKS

Dress to impress at **Jar Cocktail Club**, where a slick dress code and a lineup of DJs from across the country set the stage for a baller night out for the young and the young at heart.

GREEN (HOUSE) WITH ENVY

At **GreenHouse** the ambiance is as delightful as the food. Enveloped in greenery, with pots of figs, stripey vines, and big-leaf wonders adding to the charm, it's a haven of happiness topped with fancy, artful salads that leave you feeling good inside and out.

ASHLEY CURRIE
Local Expert

ASHLEY CURRIE is the founder and editor of *Urbaanite*—a publication devoted to giving a diverse view of how folks can live, work, play, and feel seen in Nashville. It's been a solid source for tourists and locals alike since 2015. *Urbaanite.com*

WHERE TO LISTEN TO MUSIC

Analog is a cool place where I have enjoyed hearing live music. Its focus is on R&B, which I like, and people are always pinging me about things outside of country music, so Analog has been great for that. It's right inside the **Hutton Hotel**, off West End Avenue, with a cool space. And, you know, valet parking, that's always a vibe.

GO-TO DINNER SPOTS

For great food and sometimes live music, it's **Noir Kitchen & Cocktails** in East Nashville. And I tell you, the chefs and cooks in the kitchen are absolutely amazing.

5th & Taylor is a favorite of mine in regard to atmosphere. I always say the first thing you get is the biscuit appetizer. I've never tasted biscuits like this from anywhere else—they literally melt in your mouth.

FOR BRUNCH

The **ButterFLY Garden Brunch & Events** in Lenox Village is so good. The chefs have a unique story about how they got started and their weekend brunch is the best. You have to make sure to make a reservation or you'll not get in because seating definitely fills up. They have a honey Tennessee wing. They have their shrimp and grits. They have their crab Benedict with little hush puppies. They're really great, too. Definitely get the wings with the waffle.

FINDING NEW TREATS

The **Nashville Farmers Market**, but more so the market's sheds. I love going there just to discover something new. I found a shed there that does a lot of great candles and scents. It's called the Black Candle Company, and I love them. What's great about the Nashville Farmers Market is that you can always discover someone new. There's always someone having a temporary space popping up, and they allow for that.

WHERE TO TAKE VISITORS

Oh, hands down, we're going to **Uncle Nearest** distillery in Shelbyville. We are hands down going there. You can truly make a day of it. You can go and take the tour, and then afterward you can shop and spend all your money on the great whiskey and merch. Then they have the Humble Baron bar with live music that's always so good, and they teach line dancing. It has the best drinks, best food, best music, best everything. So anytime anyone is here, we're going to go there for something.

ZONE 2

Day Trips

TO LOUISVILLE ↑

• MAMMOTH CAVES

North

🛡 24

🛡 65

• KENTUCKY LAKE

West

East

• NASHVILLE

TO KNOXVILLE →

🛡 40

• FRANKLIN

• BURGESS FALLS

🛡 40

• FALL CREEK FALLS

← TO MEMPHIS

• NATCHEZ TRACE PARKWAY

South

🛡 24

🛡 65

TO CHATTANOOGA →

North

Prepare for journeys that blend the eerie, the adventurous, and the awe-inspiring. Places where history and the supernatural intertwine. Where serene nature meets LED technology via watercraft. Little towns with historic hubs and subterranean mysteries. Plus the world's longest cave system?! Lazy Saturdays are looking up.

WITCHY WOMAN

Like all good ghost stories, there are many variations of just what the &%$ happened at the **Historic Bell Witch Cave**, but the important thing is—they are all terrifying. The story is famous upon famous, perhaps once the most widely publicized ghost story in America. Ghost hunting shows also say this place is ground zero for paranormal activity. It was even made into a Donald Sutherland/Sissy Spacek film, *An American Haunting*, which you should absolutely cuddle-watch the night before you go to get mentally prepared for all that you're about to get into.

    The Bells were a family who were haunted from 1817 to 1820 by the self-proclaimed Bell Witch. A letter from the family found years later states that there was a demon in the house and that the folks would sit waiting for the witch ghost. Richard Bell's diary lists the constant hauntings—from noises and disembodied voices to regular instances of his youngest sister being constantly physically beaten by the ghost until she was knocked out. After being threatened, the family patriarch, John Bell, was found poisoned one morning with a mysterious vial next to him. The family claims that the Bell Witch laughed and said she had given him a dose. After an investigation by the state government, the cause of death was attributed to the supernatural—a first of its kind. All in all, super creepers!

NO
- SMOKING
- CLIMBING
- RUNNING
- CRAWLING
- FOOD or DRINK

DANGER
- HIGH VOLTAGE
- LOOSE FOOTING
- LOW OVERHEAD

You can see the replica of the Bell's hewn wooden home kitted out to look as it did during their years of terror. And then you descend into the Bell Witch's cave, her supposed hang zone between wreaking havoc and where many a person has claimed to hear her eerie voice. If you really want to up the fear factor, you could take one of their lantern-only tours that also come with all the unexplained photographs of spirits taken over the years.

GLOW JOB

How often do you get to spend the day looking at doe-eyed deer and then also raving on a lake? If the answer is never, we're about to change that for you. Pack that picnic basket with all the lovely snacky things. We're talking crusty bread, we're talking fancy olives, we're talking cheese *and* jams. Then head up to **Bledsoe Creek State Park** for a loaded day. Leave the treats in the car for a bit and set out on the **Shoreline Trail**. It's an easy breezy two-mile walk around the, you guessed it, shoreline of **Old Hickory Lake**. Right away you'll notice loads of fisherfolk around the man-made lake because this is a hot spot for those who partake. Largemouth bass are the name of the fishing game here, but ol' timers will tell you how the heaviest walleye on record was caught here in 1960. All twenty-five pounds of it.

After you've done your ramblin', spread out your treats at one of the picnic tables and enjoy the time in nature. There are great blue herons, bald eagles,

and ospreys soaring through the sky to point out with wonder.
Note: a little game of Uno right about now never
hurt anyone, either (except those that keep
getting the &%$@ Draw Four cards). Before
you know it, it's time for the next round of
excitement with a Sunset/Glow Tour from
Get Up and Go Kayaking. You two will
embark on a tour inside a clear kayak, paddling along the tree-lined shores and rocky
cliffs as the sun sets brilliantly to the west.
The most romantic of romantic to-dos comes
at dusk, when the LED lights of your little vessel
shine in festive colors as you go for a moonlit paddle
on the lake. As the sun goes down and the croaking frogs come
out, row up to some turtles and look for hopping fish. Pack some raver-style
glow-in-the-dark bracelets to crack, activate, and slap on your wrists. Continue
on under the stars, tracking your lover by the neon bits moving over the calm
water. This one is real special, so save it for someone who deserves it.

HORSING AROUND

If you've never been to the tiny town of Horse Cave, Kentucky (population
two thousand and some change), go ahead and add it to the day trip list. Its
cute-as-a-button downtown district boasts more than fifty buildings listed on
the National Register of Historic Places with colorful awnings and Victorian
gingerbread. And right smack-dab in the middle of it all is a massive opening
to the **Hidden River Cave**. It's not too often you can go spelunking and do
some window shopping at little Americana brick-and-mortars, but that's just
what's on offer here. In fact, there's a whole cave museum if you really wanna
get into the subterranean aspect of Kentucky, or you can just get to it with the
adventure part. An enormous natural cave entrance with greenery all around
the steps invites you to climb down and down until, lo and behold, you are
met with near blackness. And there it is—the world's longest underground
suspension bridge, which could either sound fun to you or trigger a panic
attack (no right answer here). Also you're bound to see little critters. Again, fun
or panic. You decide. The guides will let you in on interesting tidbits such as

how this chronically water-full cave led to the town becoming one of the first in the nation to have fire hydrants. Bust that fun fact out at a dinner party!

Speaking of food, while you're in the area, you're gonna want to pay a visit to **Farmwald's Dutch Bakery and Restaurant**. The Amish-owned establishment is known for its baking skillz. Every morning they begin at three a.m., kneading and sifting and punching dough to bring their pillowy creations to the masses. Whether that's a made-to-order sandwich on fresh sourdough, a crimped Amish fried hand pie oozing with hot peach juices, or a maple bar squishy enough to have its own fanbase—it's of critical importance that you carb up. And it wouldn't hurt to buy a jar of homemade preserves before you go, either.

WHAM, BAM, THANK YOU MA'AMMOTH

If **Mammoth Cave** was a student, it'd be the teacher's pet for sure. Let's list some of its overachiever facts, shall we? It's the world's longest known cave system at 426 explored miles. It's Kentucky's oldest tourist attraction. It's an International Biosphere Reserve, a UNESCO World Heritage Site, and, as a certified International Dark Sky Park, a stargazing haven. Whew!

With fifty-three thousand acres of forests and riverways up top and a winding limestone labyrinth wonder below, there's no shortage of activities here. On the Captain Obvious front, there's a variety of cave tours from the simple to the arduous. All with 350-million-year-old rocks to ogle and weirdo little creatures who've adapted to the dark, such as cave salamanders, eyeless fish, and an endangered albino cave shrimp! If, for some reason, you get sick of cave vibes, aboveground also offers all kinds of nature hikes on wooden walkways through the forest, with birds chirping happily. Plus loads more mammals to peep at, such as the sweet Bambi-lookalike white-tailed deer, actual pack rats (properly known as Allegheny woodrats), and, once in a blue moon, coyotes or American black bears.

Point being, if you two need to get away from the computer screens, stress, the pile of dishes in the sink, etc., this is a day trip to reset the brain. And remember we're all just little ants on a spinning orb flying through space.

East

For a state nowhere near an ocean, Tennessee offers a constant stream of water activities. From the eighty waterfalls (some even in caves!) sprinkled across the state for swimming and paddling to lakes for zippy boating—water fun is on the menu. And when you get pruney, there are more hikes to eye up (and then more water). Plus a state fair to rival all others, especially on the quirky competitions front.

FALLING FOR YOU

The Volunteer State has many things in overwhelming supply—hats, hot sauce, and fireflies to name a few—but one of the most special commodities of all is its waterfalls. With more than eighty falls constantly gushing across the state, there is always a place to drive off to together and ogle the magical mist as it hits the sunlight, instantly creating your own personal rainbow. A quick google of **Tennessee Waterfall Loop** will give you a few different route options, but we like *The Tennessean*'s, which covers ten waterfalls across four different state parks. Now, technically, it's a five-ish hour loop to drive it straight, but that obviously doesn't account for all the time actually *enjoying the waterfalls*. So opt for the turtle over the hare method and tick off these beauties one by one in all the different ways. Here's three of our faves not to miss:

Swimming at Cummins

We know folks have dunked their bodies into the wondrous waters of **Cummins Falls** for thousands of years at a bare minimum, because who wouldn't want to kiss their partner in the cascading picturesque waters? This may be one of our favorite swims in the whole state, but it's made all the sweeter by the effort to get here.

Once you arrive at the 306-acre day-use park, psych yourselves up for a journey. First up, a hike that rangers deem "strenuous" on an uneven natural path through the gorge. Once your thighs are burning, you'll arrive at the river, and now you'll need to hike another 0.6 miles *through* waters that can run ankle to waist high over slippery rocks. Old tennis shoes or proper rugged water shoes are ideal here so you don't bust a toe on a surprise underwater boulder, and a waterproof backpack will really set you up for success. (In case you haven't picked up on this yet, it's not exactly a kiddo-friendly adventure.) Now that you've completed a journey surely on the level of a Viking or something equally bold, you're rewarded with a one-of-a-kind experience that *Travel + Leisure* once listed as the Tenth Best Swimming Hole in America. The Blackburn Fork River plunges off a seventy-five-foot drop into a pool full of happy folks who've just busted their buns to bask in nature together. Not to get all Martha Stewart about it, but "it's a good thing."

Hiking at Fall Creek

Midway through the waterfall loop lies one of the most popular state parks—**Fall Creek Falls**—with nearly thirty thousand acres of nature waiting for you. This park has it all. We're talking virgin hardwood timber, giant gorges, idyllic streams, and, of course, waterfalls. Yes, it has more than one. **Piney Falls**, **Cane Creek Falls**, and **Cane Creek Cascades** are all within the boundaries, but the aforementioned Fall Creek Falls is your primary destination. Standing at 256 feet, it's one of the tallest waterfalls found in the eastern part of the country, and it's equivalent to looking at a twenty-three-story high-rise that's constantly gushing gazillions of gallons of water. This is one of the easier waterfalls to ogle in the area. You can choose to just admire it and its powerful white noise sounds from the observation deck, or you can take a short 0.4-mile hike down to the base for a different view of its waters tumbling over rocks in a way that would make a helluva flume ride in another universe. But do be aware that the 0.4-mile hike down is fairly easy breezy, but going back up can leave some regretting their life choices. It's okay, though, because there are loads of other leisurely hiking trails throughout the massive park.

While some of the other waterfall adventures lend themselves to a summertime activity (i.e., getting into the water), this park is great year-round and particularly beautiful in the fall with the leaves changing and the bird-watching particularly banging. Depending on which trail you take, some of the elegantly named flying friends you might spot include the yellow-billed cuckoo, the worm-eating warbler, and the white-breasted nuthatch.

You'll surely need a break after all that good nature walking, so pop into the Lodge to find **The Restaurant at Fall Creek Falls**. Whether it's sharing artichoke dip and a burger (including a veggie option) in one of the cute plaid booths inside or clinking two copper mugs of Memphis Mules on the balcony overlooking all the greenery, it's worth the visit to round out the day.

Kayaking at Burgess

This one is an adventure date. And how do we best prepare for an adventure? With a methodical packing list! In this case it's lunch, snacks, sunscreen, reusable water bottles, and closed-toe shoes that'll make your day sink or swim because we're off to kayak at **Burgess Falls**.

There are a few options for outfitters, but one to try is **Kayaking Adventures of Tennessee**. Married duo Tara and Eddie run the company with their signature bright pink bus (complete with a kayaking cartoon cat named Patches emblazoned on the side). They'll get you loaded up with kayaks, paddles, and life vests before you set out to the falls. Then they'll guide you past murky waters and through a forest of dead tree stumps as if you're a Plinko chip getting dropped onto a game on *The Price Is Right* (if you are old enough to have watched this game show while staying home sick from school, it's time to take your calcium supplement). Keep an eye

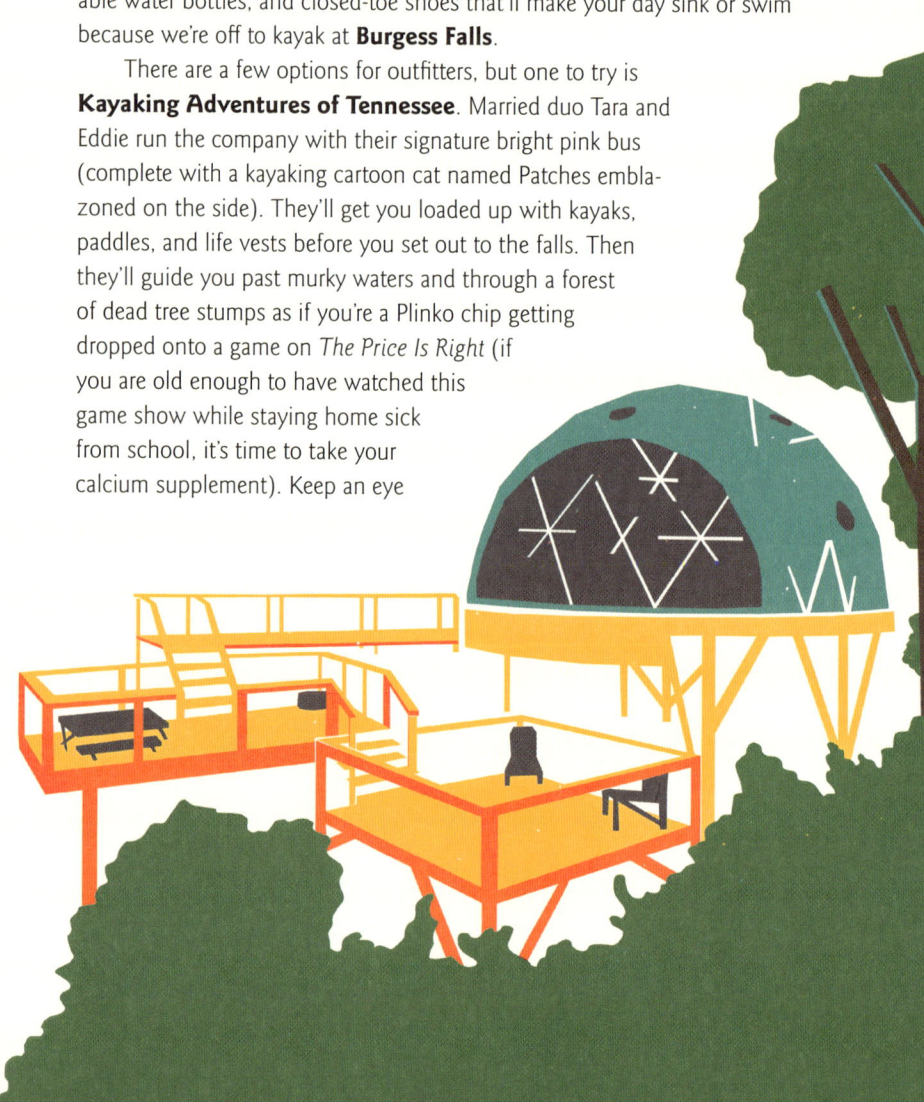

out for all sorts of stunning wildlife, from river otters to bald eagles to turtles perched on downed branches.

An hour-ish in, you'll come to the most majestic of the four falls (one with the old remains of a suspension bridge!) within the state park. You can only access the base by kayak, and when you pull up to water crashing down a stunning 130-foot cliff into a limestone gorge, you'll surely do a cartoonish double take to make sure it's all real. The land here has long impressed people with its power. It was originally a hunting ground for the Cherokee, Creek, and Chickasaw tribes in the area. And in the '30s and '40s, it generated hydroelectric power for the nearby city of Cookeville.

Depending on the level of gushing, you can either walk straight up into the glory of the falls and use it as a shower or scramble around the cliff and watch the mermaid-inclined folks backflip into the pool. Pause to scarf some of your packed lunch and re-up the SPF, then get on in again. Paddle an hour back into the setting sun and feel chuffed that you've just knocked something off most people's bucket lists. And you did it together.

You can easily call this adventure a day and head back to the city, but let's say you're not quite ready to say goodbye to the views or the wildlife. Turn it into an overnighter at **Your Glamping Adventure**. Grab yourself a dome that resembles a snow globe in the woods, complete with kitchen, comfy bed, and a view to remember. And if that isn't enough to get your snuggle on, what about a private hot tub outside your dome with a view of the stars?

PARK LIFE

Lush forest is all around as you climb the crooked stone steps to a little castle built in the 1800s. Inside a stone turret, with a canopy of trees above it, is the reservoir pump to draw water for your daily needs. This is **Spring Castle** and it is cottagecore at its finest. Built when the nearby textile mill was still active (and in need of quick access to water should a fire break out), it's fed by a crystal clear underground spring that burbles up right behind it.

If that cutie patootie building got you revved up, go ahead and bop a few feet over to the almost as old **"Minnow Box" Springhouse**. This one is attributed to when the Tennessee Electric Power Company operated the dam in the area. A fun fact about these little spring houses is that they didn't just bring something to drink to the workers and residents; the cool water also acted as a refrigerator of sorts for the structures. You can easily picture turn-of-the-century

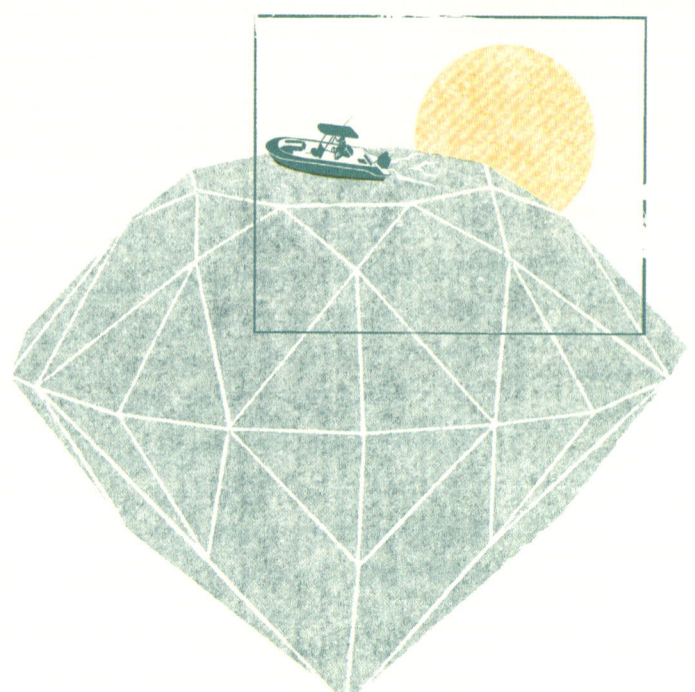

neighbors neatly stacking their crocks of butter and milk into the corners to keep them cool under the summer sun. For the official record, the state says, "Don't drink the water." For the unofficial record, some say that it's the best water they've ever tasted.

This isn't the only water to behold while visiting **Rock Island State Park**. The 883-acre park has the requisite waterfalls with out-of-this-world overlooks. And for couples who get toasty on their wanders, hit the sandy swim beach for an easy dip. Reward your bodies for spending time in nature by prepacking a primo picnic (cold pizza packed in a cooler is delicious, FWIW) and stretching out at one of the tables here.

HOT TIP: When the wildflowers start blooming in springtime, this place looks like a page straight out of a fairytale picture book. Plan accordingly because the crowds will be there to look, too.

DREAMBOAT

There are boat people and then there are *boat people*. And the latter have all sorts of responsibilities associated with the role—maintaining said boat, parking it, saluting each other, etc. But the first type of boat people just love to occasionally get onto the water and shout, "I feel the need, the need for speed" while wind whips through their hair. Those folks might want to entertain the idea of a boat membership at **Freedom Boat Club**. To make it worth the initiation fee and monthly dues, you have to be super into the idea and ideally have a crew of friends who also love going out. Let the FBC handle all maintenance and storage plus you'll get unlimited training from certified captains on their fleet of boats that you can reserve online.

Technically they have eleven locations all around the state, including one at the **Center Hill Marina & Yacht Club**. Take off in the waters for a zoom around, watch a seaplane awkwardly take off like a gangly flamingo heading for flight, and stretch out in a donut-shaped floatie where appropriate. And after a day of sun is over, the **El Lago Mexican Restaurant** is right at the marina beckoning to you because even a great day can be made better by adding chips and salsa to it.

TIGHT SQUEEZE

This locale is pretty cute from the second you pull up, with a little rock stream and a teeny pond with lily pads, before you even get to what lies below. As you descend 333 feet into the **Cumberland Caverns**, some of the thoughts that might flit across your brain are, "Whoa, it's colder than I thought in here," "I feel like an ant in this huge space," and "Is that a bat?!"

It's the second longest cave in the state, at over twenty-seven miles, and full of spelunking magic. It's a little creepy what with being trapped below the surface and stalagmites and 'tites giving off melting alien vibes. But it's also stunning with underground waterfalls, glittering pools, and a light show of pinks and oranges melting into blues and greens. They even have a lovely amphitheater area deep down with an elegant chandelier formerly from Loew's Metropolitan Theatre in New York. And above all else, it's surely a way to mix up the same ol' same ol'.

FAIR PLAY

The **Wilson County Tennessee State Fair** is a mouthful to say and a mouthful to visit. We're talking buttered-up cobs of corn, deep-fried PB&Js, Tennessee Tatercakes, and high piles of shaved ice all up for grabs. Far too many of the rides spin round and round (especially if you've consumed much of the aforementioned), such as the Tilt-A-Whirl, Zero Gravity, and the Zipper. But for the timid fun seekers: can we interest you in the innocence of the Super Fun Slide? Even if all these are your version of a nightmare, it's somehow fun to watch others' faces contort with fear and glee.

Like all good American institutions there's a healthy bit of competition at play with a Zucchini Bread contest (baking, not eating) and a Hair vs. Hare contest, where you try to match your salt and pepper locks to one of the cute bunnies on site (winner gets a plaque!). And the most surprising of all is an actual Husband Calling contest where ladies stand atop a stage decorated with folksy hand-assembled quilts and take turns high hollering for their men. See a competitor summon all the air possible into a diaphragm and yell out names like *Jerrrrrryyyyyyyyyyy! Heeeeerrrrrreeeee Hoooooooowwwwwwwwiiiieeeeeeeeeeee!* to an audience and a panel of judges who tilt their heads quizzically and some-how determine which of them is superior. 'Merica!

South

Picture this: Unwinding at a high-end spa, strolling through a quaint small town that could easily grace a postcard, or sipping wine with your feet dipped in a cool creek. Then you kick things up with a killer music festival and a nod to the man who gave us Tennessee whiskey. We've got that and more in our southern outskirts. Let's go.

HOT AND STEAMY

Life is hard and sometimes it's best counteracted with a day of indulgence and not a whisper of the thing that's causing anxiety. So the next time your partner is eyeballsdeep in a stress coma, whisk them away for this day of relaxation. It may not fix all their problems, but forgetting them for an afternoon sure will help.

So get thee to a day at the **Southall Farm & Inn**! Begin at the spa with all manner of things to make that constantly furrowed brow and tension migraine dissipate. Book a day pass for access to an instant trip to the stress-melting sauna and steam room. Then slip into the steaming-hot outdoor mineral pool with chaise lounges, allowing you to take in the pleasing view of some of the little lake and the 325 acres of farmland. Some folks claim

breathing in the salty mineral air has a host of health benefits, from lowering inflammation to improving respiratory conditions and skin health. Plus chilling out the nervous system and helping with a better night's sleep. All we know is it definitely feels good.

Then cuddle up in robes as soft as your childhood stuffed animal and relax in candlelit lounges with beds to sit on to finally calm your racing mind. And no bougie spa lounge would be complete without scrumptious snacks such as little cookies and dried fruit. After you're as blissed out as Gwyneth Paltrow at a high-end yoga retreat, move to the next phase of nurturing the body—healthy food.

At their on-site restaurant, **January** (reservations required), you'll find a menu full of grown-right-here options served in a room straight out of the pages of a design magazine. The prices are on par with how fancy you'll feel, but treating yourself is worth it. You can call it a lovely day right there and head home, but if the wallet and the heart are both in sync with your desire to make it an overnighter, that'll just extend the bliss.

JEEPERS LEIPERS

The village of Leiper's Fork must have been created in a lab by the same execs who make Hallmark movies. Its teeny one-horse-town feel, with a population of 650, is protected by The Land Trust for Tennessee, so while the rest of the world keeps changing, it won't. It doesn't take long to investigate the handful of properties, but it is a nice wander. The artistic hub has an outsized ratio of galleries for its size, with something for all tastes.

At **Leiper's Creek Gallery** you can behold sculptures and expressionist paintings inside a quaint-looking cabin complete with a front firepit. Out back they have a "lawn chair theater" with fun things for the community such as summer movies for the kids or music acts traveling through. Inside a pictur-esque 1860s home is fine artisan heaven, **The Copper Fox Gallery**. In one little space they display pottery, handmade furniture, and blown glass from ninety artists across the Southeast.

Come summer, amp up this date to Hallmark times one thousand with a reservation at one of the **Farmstead Roots Creek Dinner Series at Wines in the Fork**. What is that, you ask? Only possibly the most romantic date idea we've encountered in all our travels. You and your sweetie will sit at a long table erected *in the creek*. Yes, that's right. On a hot Tennessee night, your feet are in the cool water of the creek, twinkling lights overhead and live music wafting from the banks while you eat a multicourse family-style meal prepared by noted local chefs and paired with their signature wines. Truly this is a ren-dezvous like no other.

QUITE FRANKLIN

Founded in 1799 and named after notoriously sketchy kite flyer Benjamin Franklin, the town of Franklin is pretty dang cute. The sixteen-block historic district includes buildings from the Federal, Victorian, and Art Deco eras, now full of bustling shoppers and visitors. Pop inside the **Frothy Monkey** cafe, located inside the former Historic Franklin Presbyterian Church, for lunch or a fancy coffee drink. Then get to window-shopping down the way, popping into anything that grabs your eye, such as **White's Mercantile** with shelves stocked with all manner of colorful trinkets from jewelry to journals to "White Paw" dog toys.

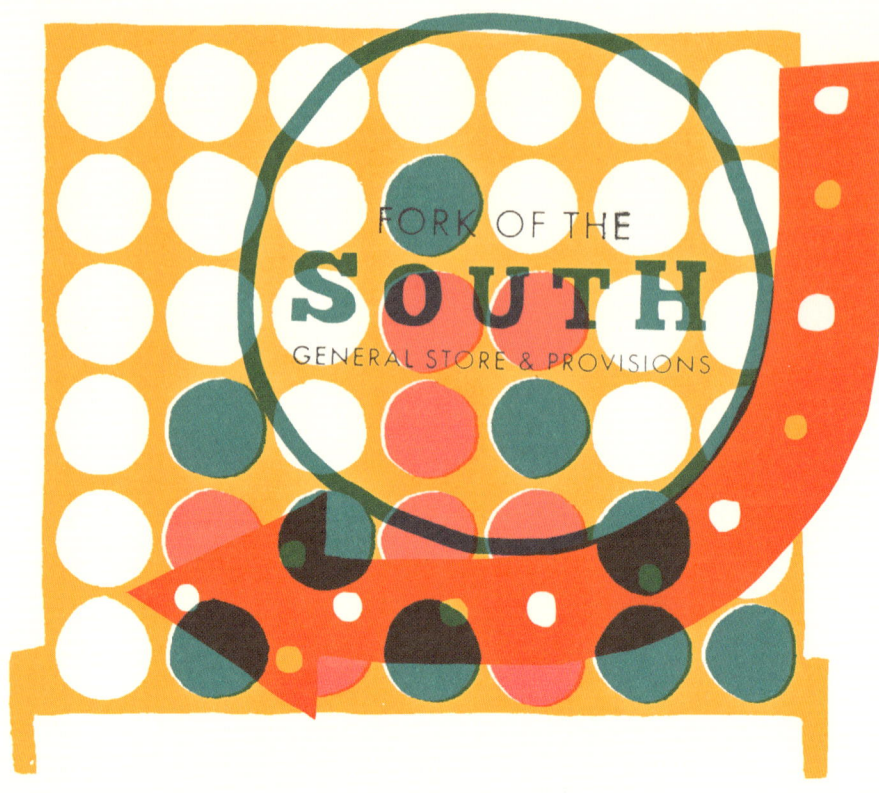

One to hit is **Rooted from Yarrow Acres** because, as the old saying goes, "take someone to a plant store to show them you like them." Pink-embellished leaves of the calathea and a shelf of tiny "Feed me, Seymour!" carnivorous fly traps beside atriums and "Plant Hippy" T-shirts. If you want your heartthrob to remember you, get them a plant so they think of you daily. If they kill it . . . maybe it was never meant to be.

Then off to **The Factory at Franklin**. What was once a 1929 stove factory is now a lively center of indie shops, vintage stores, live music, and delicious things to put in your mouth. Channel your inner Bob Ross at **Third Coast Clay** by selecting a plain little ceramic planter with mushrooms or a garden gnome from the shelves to artistically paint up to your heart's content and leave behind to get fired to perfection. Then consider a stop into **Fork of the South** to pick up one of their tiny pocket-sized games of Simon or Sorry! Complete the day by playing a round of your newly acquired miniature game in the airy food court with a scoop of Burnt Orange Dreamsicle from **Jeni's Splendid Ice Creams** because it matches the day you've just had.

DRIVING ME WILD

Start your day by indulging at **Loveless Cafe**, a local institution that's served loads of famous faces (check their photo wall!) and regulars alike. Known for its legendary biscuits, each fluffy bite paired with homemade strawberry preserves is a little piece of heaven for those celebrating, commiserating, or just plain hungry. Play a game of cornhole to let the catfish settle and get ready to hop into the car for a drive up the **Natchez Trace Parkway**. This 444-mile scenic road has witnessed ten thousand years of travel, trade, and transformation. It's seen the high highs and utter lows of human history, but today it's a peaceful escape from the hustle of daily life. The parkway winds through three states, offering up some of the most picturesque views you'll find anywhere.

As you cruise along put on your favorite playlist and settle into the rhythm of the drive. If it's autumn the trees will treat you to a spectacle—fiery reds from beta-carotene and golden yellows from flavanols—painting the landscape in warm hues. Drive until you reach the **Gordon House**, an album's worth of time away at milepost 363, where you can pull over to stretch your legs by one of the few buildings along the trail. Songbirds and woodpeckers flutter in the trees, and it's a good deep breath before you put on another album and head back, mind and heart cleared.

NEAREST AND DEAREST

Casual whiskey drinkers around the world likely have no idea how much they owe their *Cheers* to a man named Nathan "Nearest" Green, aka Uncle Nearest. In the mid-1800s he was an enslaved man working on a farm in the hills above Lynchburg, perfecting the art of producing Tennessee whiskey by filtering it through charcoal made from sugar maple trees—a process likely passed down from West African tradition, where folks filtered their water through charcoal to purify it.

He continued working on that farm after becoming a free man and, during his time, made one of the greatest impacts on the world of whiskey. He famously mentored a young boy who came to the farm, taking him under his

wing and teaching him all he knew. Eventually that boy would repay Nearest for his kindness by making him the first African American master distiller on record. That boy was Jack Daniel.

You can learn more about the Godfather of Tennessee Whiskey at the 270-acre **Nearest Green Distillery** property and get a chance to taste some of the most awarded whiskey there is. You can admire the photos and antiques on display, view the bottling house and gorgeous sunsets, enjoy their on-site barbecue, and, of course, buy all manner of whiskey-related treats to take home.

BEE IN YOUR BONNAROO

The east coast gets the legend of Woodstock. The west coast claims the desert vibes of Coachella. But everyone in between flocks to the seven-hundred-acre Great Stage Park in Manchester each June for the one and only **Bonnaroo** music festival. There are multiple reasons why it's been called the "Festival of the Decade" by *Consequence of Sound* and labeled one of the best music festivals by *Rolling Stone*, *Spin*, and even the Grammys. Its commitment to sustainability, its summer camp nostalgia feeling, its nonstop funtivities around the estate when your ears need a break from the speakers. There are daily free yoga classes with your feet in the grass, a famous mushroom fountain, a ginormous inflatable waterslide to stay cool, and parades of costumed concertgoers aplenty.

But at the top of the list, making this festival so beloved, is the curation. Every year there's something to get psyched about, whether it's D'Angelo's return to the stage after a decade hiatus or the final Beastie Boys show ever played. Plus the eclectic roster that means you just might see the Flaming Lips, Eminem, Megan Thee Stallion, and Pearl Jam all in a weekend. That's called range, sweetie.

COLUMBIA CUTIES

It's ridiculous how many cute towns there are ripe for the itinerary plucking. Try rolling into Columbia, TN, on the **First Fridays** of the month to kick off your weekend right. We're not the only ones who have fallen for the charismatic town center a little—it's won multiple awards for being just as sweet as a Southern tea.

From April through December, on the first Fri-yays (see what we did there?), the streets start bustling with a mix of outdoor live music, food trucks wafting drool-worthy things, and a slew of local makers. Go ahead and stroll hand in hand while you scope out everything from homemade clothes to

hand-dipped caramel apples to freshly cut flowers, all while a banjo picker strums just around the corner.

Did we mention it's a spot for (car) lovers? Columbia's mini cruise-in is also part of the fun, so you can ogle vintage rides and maybe even chat up an enthusiast about that '68 Camaro they've got polished to perfection. It's a family-friendly date, too, perfect if you've got kiddos or that out-of-town family whose small-talk reserves you exhausted months ago. Everyone gets to enjoy the festive energy while you silently congratulate yourself for planning anything other than another night in front of the TV.

If your date happens to fall during **Mule Day**, well, then you've struck gold. It turns out that Columbia is the **Mule Capital of the World** and every spring, it celebrates this surprising fact with what can only be described as full-fledged hullabaloo. What started as a mule breeders' meet-up in 1840 has grown into a four-day festival that pulls in over two hundred thousand people, and yes, there's a parade—though not just any parade. Imagine mules pulling decorative floats shaped like covered wagons or, if the mood strikes, red solo cups. The real MVPs of the weekend—the mules—are celebrated with pageantry and pride, proving they're far more than just farm animals.

Events stretch all weekend and cover everything from line dancing to a dog show (yes, that's right), and you'll even stumble across a **Miss Mule Day pageant**. While some may wonder if they're crowning a two-legged or four-legged contestant, you're gonna have to make the trip to find out for yourself.

UP, UP, AND AWAY

Have you ever considered starting the day floating above the peaceful Tennessee countryside in a hot-air balloon—and feeling like you've stepped straight into a dream? You probably should. At **Gateway Hot Air Balloon Adventures** in Spring Hill, your sunrise adventure kicks off with a colorful circus tent of a balloon inflating before your eyes. Then when the sky is revealing its painted soft pinks and oranges, and just as the sun peeks over the horizon, you lift off, sailing into the morning like you've got the whole world to yourselves.

Your second-generation pilot knows exactly how to keep things smooth and safe, so all you have to do is hold tight to your partner and take in the view. Down below you'll see tiny farmhouses and endless green stretching out in every direction while you float on a gentle breeze like two little lovebirds in the sky. It's a once-in-a-lifetime experience—take a beta-blocker if you have a fear of heights—you'll treasure it for a lifetime.

DIGITAL DETOX

In 2024, US Surgeon General Dr. Vivek Murthy called on Congress to start treating social media platforms more like the side-eye emoji, stating they should come with warning labels that explain the mental health harm they may cause to young people. You know what families do not have to worry about such a thing? The 250 Amish families in Ethridge, Tennessee, who adhere to the Swartzentruber lifestyle which means no electricity, no computers, no indoor plumbing, and nary a smartphone in sight.

But they do welcome tourists in for a day to visit their way of life. That includes visits to farms and antique stores and munching on freshly baked treats. Start with a trip to the **Amish Welcome Center**. Historically they've offered horse-drawn wagon tours of the area, but that isn't always a guarantee. Regardless, you can pick up a free tourist map of the area to see which farms and shops to visit and then wave to countless horse and buggies on the road, noting large families (an average of 10 to 20 children per family!) in bonnets and plain clothes tending their farms and offering homemade jellies, sorghum molasses, canned goods captured during the peak of summer, and every manner of little whittled wood thing.

There are dozens of possible farms to visit in the area, most with signs out front detailing their specialties. Don't forget to hit the ATM before you go as Apple Pay doesn't exist here. In fact, forget your phone altogether since photos are discouraged, allowing you a moment to live technology-free, too.

WINE TIME

Sometimes we want to embrace the leisurely wine-drinking lifestyle. And rolling up to **Arrington Vineyards**, where you'll be greeted by rows upon rows of grapevines and a serotonin-inducing view, certainly makes it easy. Let us paint the picture for you: massive country homes dotting the green hills, and, if you squint, you may even spot a famous country star strumming a tune on the porch. A bunch live in the area, so why not? The vineyard boasts sixteen acres of grapes and five tasting rooms, so there's plenty of vino to sample as you stroll arm in arm, dropping all the knowledgeable buzzwords, such as "tannins," "terroir," and "bouquets."

Spring through fall, the ninety-five-acre grounds are humming with music. Performers belt tunes into the air as you settle into one of the many idyllic spots—whether it's a cozy corner near the vines or a blanket sprawled out with panoramic pastoral views. As always we encourage making a whole afternoon out of it. Arrington sells an assortment of goodies—crackers, chips, cured meats, olives, and gourmet cheeses—all perfect for creating the bougie version of your childhood Lunchables to go perfectly with your wine.

LET'S SMASH

IDK if you've noticed, butttttt the world has kind of been in a constant stream of stress for some years now. And all that tension needs somewhere to go so that we don't all self-combust or get snippy with our partners for no fault of their own. So how about this for a date—hop over to Murfreesboro and get it all out. But how, you ask?

Destroy Some *%$#

At **TN Axe and Smash**, visitors get outfitted with proper safety gear and then head into a rage room to get it on. And by "on" we mean taking a bat and smashing broken TVs, taunting Precious Moments figurines, old glassware, and a million other things into teeny shards of nothingness. You can even bring in your own stuff to smash if you have something personally weighing down your soul that would benefit from the ol' bat treatment.

Throw Weapons

Jack Split does one thing: let people throw axes. One of their, *ahem*, axeperts will show you the right way to grip a handle and send your steel blade flying down a lane toward a wall target. You'd be surprised just how much hitting a bull's-eye with a sharp edge feels like a great talk therapy sesh.

Bounce House

House of Pain knew what they were talking about in the wizened lyrics of "Jump Around." Because bouncing around can actually cure what ails you. Prove it by doing all manner of diving into things at **Sky Zone**. Here it's easy to cosplay as *American Gladiators* (who all had great names, such as Blaze and Nitro) on their quirky courses. They have Boulder Balls to balance on, a Tug

Of War station over a foam pit, a trampoline to fly off and into a mountain of squishy blocks, and even a whole freaking Ninja Warrior Course. You'll be too tired to ever fight again.

Get Naked

Okay, okay. Admittedly this one isn't for everyone, but maybe stripping off the clothes would strip off some of the stress of the world too? If you feel game to give it a try, or maybe you're already a nudie pro, you can opt for a trip to the **Rock Haven Lodge Family Nudist Park**. If you like lively pastimes, they got them all on this sprawling thirty-acre estate, complete with wee little cabins and camping sites. That means swimming and soaking in a hot tub, as well as playing volleyball, shuffleboard, darts, Ping-Pong, pool, horseshoes, tennis, and pickleball. All with your pickles out.

More Fun

PAR-TEA TIME Spend a delightful *Downton Abbey*–like day by reserving the **Afternoon Tea** at **Nashville Tea Company**. It's like the pretend tea parties of childhood came alive for the full deal with a piping hot pot next to their house-made scones, jams, and sweet creams. Plus all the tea cakes and finger sandwiches one could want.

FINGER FUN Two blocks off Franklin's Main Street is **The Legendary Kimbro's Pickin' Parlor**. It is an unassuming little historic home from the outside, while inside each room offers a different spot to watch a never-ending stream of talent from a five-piece jam band to a solo songstress.

ANIMAL FARM Got 🧒 kids who like 🦙 kids? Take them to the **Lucky Ladd Farms,** where sixty acres of petting zoos, nature trails, and hundreds of pretty birdies in an aviary await. Plus all the fun seasonal farm things like tulip fields and an epic pumpkin patch. Oh, and don't forget the Enchanted Fairytale Festival with "unicorn" pony rides!

SUGAR RUSH Every third Saturday in June, get thyself to the Bell Buckle Chamber of Commerce–hosted **RC Cola-MoonPie Festival**. Yes, it's about drinking an ice-cold cola and chomping a gooey-centered pie, but the town blows it out with 5Ks, crowning a King and Queen of the fest, and of course, cutting into the world's largest MoonPie for all to share.

West

Sometimes you forget just how lucky you are to live in such a stunning, nature-filled state. Tennessee boasts pristine waterfalls, lush forests, and more biodiversity than most. So grab your love, head outside, and enjoy these natural treasures together. From biking to hiking and floating to horseback riding, there is no shortage of ways to fill your happy days.

AN APPRECIATION
INTERLUDE

You know you have a postcard-worthy state, but like all other relationships, sometimes we take things for granted. And it's important to occasionally remember just how lucky you are to be near so many trees, waterfalls, and beautiful walks. Restaurants will close, budgets will fluctuate, and tastes will change, but nature dates will always be there. So let's brag about the Volunteer State's stats for just a moment, shall we? It's in the top third of all states for biodiversity and in the top three for amphibian diversity, with 21 frog species and 56 salamander species (hot!). There are 130 species of trees in the Great Smoky Mountains, so that area alone has more types than *all* of Northern

Europe (suck it, Baltic Sea coastline!). And as the number one producer of hardwood flooring, Tennessee is the "Hardwood Capital of the World" (no joke even needed on this one).

So pat your honey on the buns and say, "We're going off to enjoy the world today," and then get on it with one of these adventures.

HOT TO TROT

Keep that relationship healthy as a horse by, um, riding one? Or maybe take the reins on your relationship with a guided horseback trail ride. Either way, you can try a hobby horse (we've run out of horse puns now) from **Natchez Trace Stables**. Whether you're an experienced rider or someone who's never seen *Seabiscuit*, this family-owned business welcomes riders of all levels. For over twenty years they've helped folks enjoy nature from atop their friendly stallions. You'll follow tree-covered trails, cross shallow creeks, and take in the rolling green hills of Tennessee's countryside. Most folks opt for the two-hour ride—just enough time to experience the peaceful scenery while forging a bond with your trusty steed. It's a perfect date for those who want to slow down and take in nature from a whole new perspective. Bonus: the reviews for this place are filled with love for both the beautiful horses and the kind folks who run it.

FLOAT ON

Grab your friends and lazy-style your way down the **Harpeth River** with **Sunshine's Adventures's tubing setup**. You don't need to be a pro—just show up, pay the fee, and let the river take care of the rest. Their three-mile route from **Newsom's Mill** to **Hidden Lake** takes anywhere from four to six hours, depending on how much you paddle versus how much you let the current do the work. Pro tip: You can sip fizzy drinks, laugh at each other's tube-fumbling attempts, and point out turtles (who probably think you're zooming by). The tubes are decked out with backrests and cup holders, and your life vest is included, so just kick back and enjoy the flow.

SHOEGAZE

For a date that gets your creative juices flowing, head to **The Walls Art Park**, a unique outdoor gallery where nature meets art, *dahling*. Unlike a regular museum, where they firmly discourage participation, here you are invited to

join in with making the art. Grab some spray cans and let your inner *artiste* loose. The rules are simple: keep it family-friendly, date your creation, and don't cover any art less than thirty days old. It's all part of the fun—whether you're admiring murals or adding your own masterpiece. Some works of art will make you stop in awe, while others might have you scratching your head. It's all very Andy Warhol when he said, "They always say time changes things, but you actually have to change them yourself."

BIKER GANG

Get those legs pumping with a leisurely ride along the **Clarksville Greenway**—an old, abandoned railway-turned-scenic-bike-trail. Stretching for nine miles, the paved path is perfect for all levels of bikers and surrounded by lush greenery in every imaginable shade—emerald, moss, hunter—you name it. Along the way, you'll whiz past creeks, bluffs, and fields of wildflowers, with scenic views to stop and snap photos of whenever you need a breather. Make sure to take in the six-hundred-foot bridge, a highlight of the trail offering stunning vistas that make the ride even more rewarding.

NATURE AND NURTURE

We owe this delightful afternoon to the foresight of Dr. Evangeline Bowie, who bought a ginormous, barren plot of land in the 1950s and then got to work building terraces, digging lakes, and planting over five hundred thousand loblolly pine trees, eventually bestowing the collective us with **Bowie Nature Park**. All that backbreaking work now means that cute couples get seventeen miles of winding trails that move the traveler through ecosystems galore—wetlands, grasslands, an oak and hickory forest, a pine forest, and even some lowland bottom wetlands. You can talk and admire pretty leaves for hours and hours. A great date choice for when you've got things to discuss.

SWIM FAN

Less than two hours away from bustling downtown Nashville are the placid waters of **Kentucky Lake**. Sure from the science perspective, you can call it a "160,309-acre reservoir created for flood control and hydroelectric power," but from a *fun* perspective, you can call it "limitless." One option is to rent a pontoon boat from **Paris Landing Pontoon Rental** at Old 76 Harbor. Grab one of those beauties with some friends, tootle out away from everyone else, and hop into the waters for a grand ol' swim with buffalo carp flitting around your toes.

TAKE A HIKE

It's nice when a hike begins with a gorgeous drive from the city. It cues the brain that this is gonna be a delightful time, and that's exactly what the **Narrows of the Harpeth** is. There are three hikes to choose from at the common trailhead without a dud in the bunch. One half-mile jaunt involves a bit of bun busting to get to the bluff and look out over the whole world with a panoramic view. There's also a half-mile trail on the backside of the bluffs, which leads to a small waterfall at the site of an old iron forge that also holds the oldest man-made tunnels in existence today. History! Round out the day with a stop at **The Yorkshire Deli** with its tearoom menu to let the legs de-jelly. The Brit owners have made this place as cute as can be, with colorful umbrellas dotting the outside. Say hello to the chickens and then order up some bangers and mash or buttery crumpets along with a perfect pot of tea.

magic STARTS HERE

tea time

ZONE 3
Overnighters

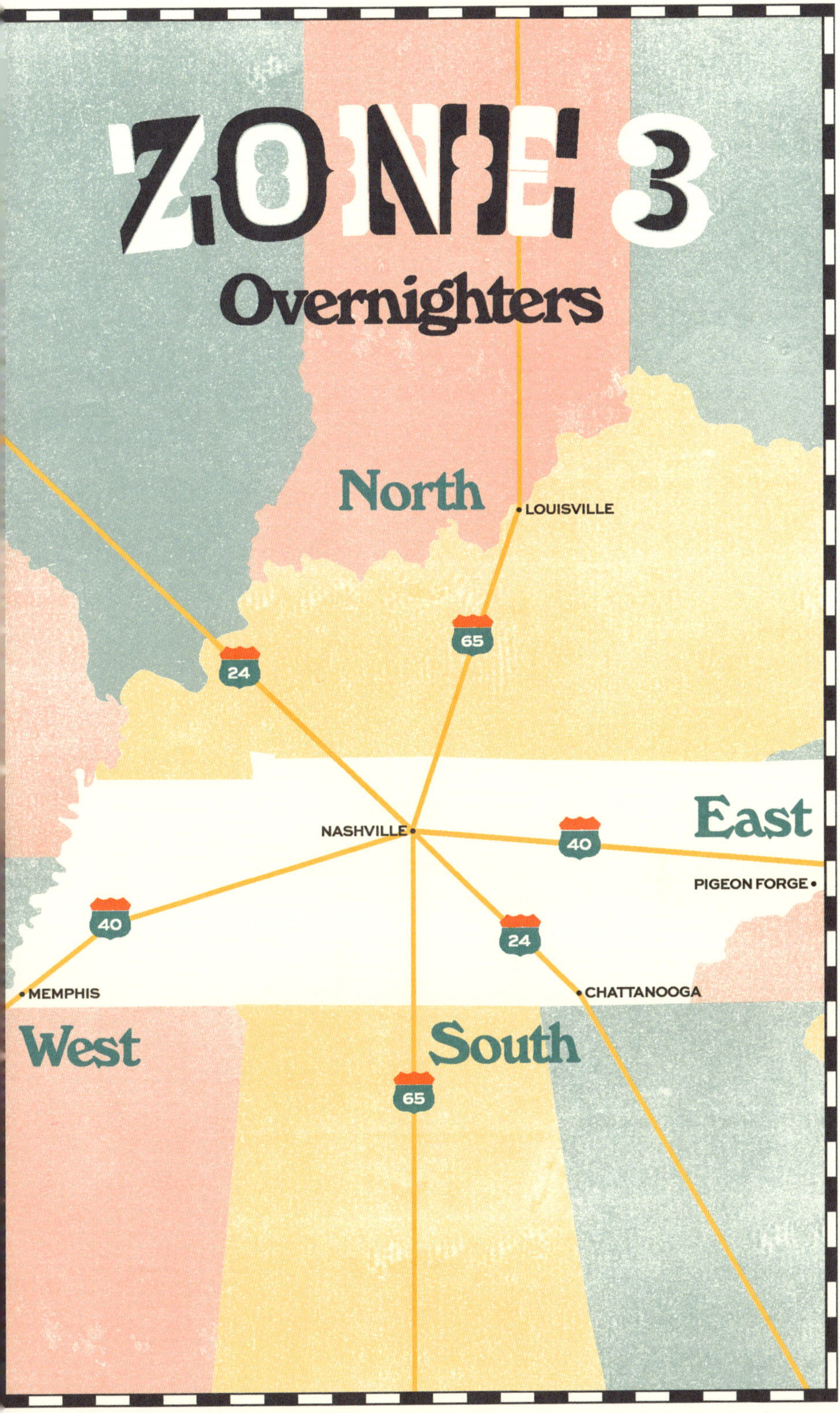

North

• LOUISVILLE

24

65

East

NASHVILLE •

40

PIGEON FORGE •

40

24

West

• MEMPHIS

• CHATTANOOGA

South

65

North

Overnights to the north offer a mix of adventure, whimsy, and indulgence. Choose from the sprawling Daniel Boone National Forest, with magical sandstone arches and trails that take your breath away, and rest your head in a one-of-a-kind tree house cabin. Or opt for a weekend in Louisville, where Victorian houses, botanical gardens, and bourbon bliss abound.

INTO THE WOODS

We're heading up into the woods, people! And very big woods they are, too. The sprawling **Daniel Boone National Forest** covers over *two million acres* across twenty-one counties—making it more than two thousand times the size of New York's Central Park! As far as nature things go, you're gonna find whatever your heart wants. We're talking scenic drives, hiking trails, and historic landmarks. They've got it all. But with such a massive expanse, it's smart to start your trip at the **Gladie Visitor Center**. Not only does the center offer clean bathrooms (a crucial detail), but the knowledgeable staff can point you toward scenic overlooks and accessible drives for a more relaxed experience or a deep dive into the rich history of the park. The northern region is the historic land of the Shawnee, while the southern portion belonged to the Cherokee.

With bucket-list-worthy natural wonders scattered throughout, it's clear that a single weekend won't even scratch the surface. When we're not sure where to begin, we start with a Google image search to see what sparks the fire within. Let's start with some of the stunning hikes without a bad view among them: **Chimney Top Trail**, **Henson's Arch Trail**, **Angel Windows Trail**, and **Whistling Arch Trail** are a handful that are all worth your time to investigate.

The belle of the forest ball might be the **Red River Gorge Geological Area**, where you'll find over one hundred natural sandstone arches and towering cliffs that have surely inspired some kind of fantasy novel with elves and flying horses. As you walk beneath these breathtaking rock formations, notice the rock climbers scaling the cliffs with impressive skill and ease—like the kids who always aced the monkey bars on the playground.

After exploring the arches, head to **Natural Bridge State Resort Park** and take the **Skylift** for a pretty dang impressive view of the world.

Float above the fluffy green canopy of trees for a mile-long ride to the top, where the spectacular **Natural Bridge** awaits. This nine-hundred-ton sandstone arch—shaped by wind and water over centuries—acts as a thirty-foot-wide natural sidewalk, allowing you to walk across this massive piece of natural architecture. The panoramic views from up here are never going to be as good in photos, so take all the mental snaps you can.

For water-loving adventurers, the area offers endless ways to splash around—boating, tubing, canoeing, or even scuba diving; there's no shortage of options. Since we're all about trying something new, how about a kayak tour through a flooded underground mine? Sure, maybe you've kayaked before, but this is certainly a twist. You glide across the crystal clear waters in an equally crystal clear kayak, giving you a front row view of the rainbow trout swimming inches below your butt. To up the ooh and aah level, try upgrading to the deluxe version with underwater LED lights that transform the dark, serene waters into a glowing, ethereal party.

Obviously, after traipsing for hours under trees, over cliffs, and through water, you're going to want a cozy place to lay your head for the weekend. There are adorable cabin options aplenty in the area and several are on offer from **Red River Gorgeous**. This family biz has some unique rentals, including barrel cabins suspended from limestone cliffs, treehouses perched atop pignut hickory and tulip poplar trees, and one cutie called "the Pirate Ship." A weekend in a treehouse is surely the antidote to a life spent hunched in front of a computer, no?

LITTLE SLUGGERS

Ah, Louisville. Home of Muhammad Ali, Jennifer Lawrence, and the Slugger bat. Plus a little horse race at **Churchill Downs** called the Kentucky Derby that has kept the hat biz alive and well for 150 years. There are loads of things to do on a weekend. Some things you've likely seen on social media, such as the hundred-acre limestone **Mega Cavern**, where the powers that be once made plans in the 1960s to house fifty thousand people in case of a nuclear attack. Or the gorgeous **Belle of Louisville**—the oldest still-operating steamboat of its kind—valiantly swirling its mighty red paddles up and down the waters. It's all attention worthy, but perhaps we can tip you off to some relaxation-forward activities.

Try starting your day at **KIWA**. It's the only Korean café in town, and their seasonal menu is equally pretty and tasty, with things such as a pink Yeoi Sakura Latte and a plate of waffles artfully decorated with fruit served in the sunny dining room. Who says casual can't be elegant too? And since carbs

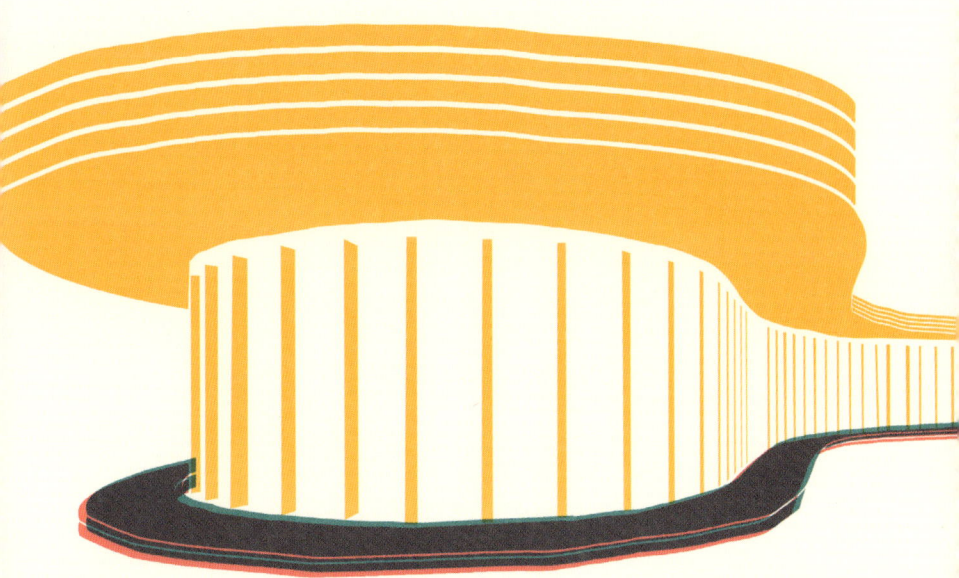

don't count if you get moving right after, pop straight over to the **Waterfront Botanical Gardens**. Once a landfill, now it's slowly becoming an urban oasis of gardens with multiple phases in progress. See pretty poppies in bloom, blue-tiled fountains, and black-eyed Susans in droves.

In fact the city is a great place to go for a walk and to ogle pretty things. Another option is a self-guided walking tour of some of the purdiest houses around. Old Louisville is championed as having the largest collection of restored Victorian homes in the country. The neighborhood, with more than forty city blocks of Victorian-era homes, was built in the 1870s, and many of its homes are still looking good today. Start in Central Park, which was once a family estate, and then begin your meander to the big stops. Google a walking tour (get a self-guided map or join a tour) to give you all the deets, but ones to not miss include the jaw-dropping **Conrad-Caldwell House** (otherwise known as **"Conrad's Castle"**) and the gorgeous French-inspired **Pink Palace**—built as the home for the "gentleman's club and casino."

EAT, DRINK, AND BE MERRY

When you're on a romantic getaway, you want the vibes to be immaculate in the evening. A long, leisurely dinner with a view definitely sets the tone. The first step is to check your phone and find out what time the sun currently sets at, and the second step is to make a reservation a half hour prior to that at **River House**. A beyond-gorgeous view of the Ohio River, with the sunset glinting off it and a fine wine in hand, is good in itself. Add their stellar menu, with items such as Maker's barrel plank smoked salmon, crispy parmesan grit cakes, and okra ratatouille (no rats steering a chef in this version), and this is a killer dinner date.

But because vacay is about going one step more, we're heading over to Whiskey Row to get down. Enter a nondescript door before descending into the speakeasy below, **Hell or High Water**, which has just about as sexy date-night vibes as they come. The room is swathed in red velvet booths, fringed lampshades, burgundy leather armchairs, and floor-to-ceiling bookshelves over-flowing with vintage hardbacks. Be sure to look for the wardrobe closet that leads to a secret room. Then order one of their curated cocktails such as the Struggle Buggy with Old Forester bourbon, lime, spiced maple, and club soda. Now snuggle up close—the velvet couch wants you to.

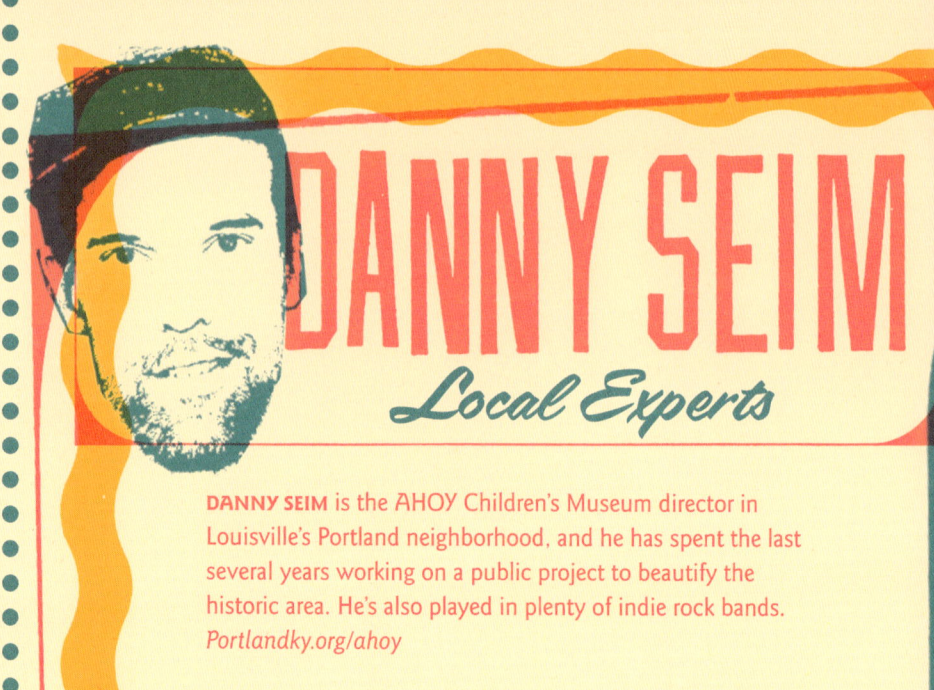

DANNY SEIM
Local Experts

DANNY SEIM is the AHOY Children's Museum director in Louisville's Portland neighborhood, and he has spent the last several years working on a public project to beautify the historic area. He's also played in plenty of indie rock bands. *Portlandky.org/ahoy*

ONE FOR THE HISTORY BOOKS

The fossil beds at **Falls of the Ohio State Park** are awesome because they're right in the middle of the river, which is a half mile out of the city. They're free. They're still unprotected, which is nuts because you can go out there at any time of the day during the summer and just walk around over these 300-million-year-old Devonian fossils that are, quite literally, underneath your feet everywhere you look. That's so cool.

A NEIGHBORHOOD FAVE

The Table restaurant in Portland is really awesome. They have this great pay-what-you-can structure, where if you're houseless and need to eat, they'll let you wash dishes to pay for meals. Or the owner told me someone might bring in a Beanie Babies collection and trade it for meals. It's really sweet, but the food is top-tier, well-prepared southern comfort food that is still at prices that don't discourage people in the neighborhood from actually eating it.

FOR THE KIDDOS

Well, the **Portland Museum** is often called a gem of Louisville, and we're very proud of that. It's been around for almost fifty years now and kind of seen as one thing for the first forty-five of those years, and now we're doing our best to breathe new life into it, update the exhibits and get more kids involved, which is a segue to this AHOY project. It's modeled after these immersive experiences that are popping up across the country—creating this kind of psychedelic wonder world where some things line up and some things don't.

A RELIABLE FAVORITE

Vietnam Kitchen is this place that's kind of so ubiquitous to the locals that no one talks about it anymore. But when we were buying our house, the people who sold it to us took us here. It's kind of far out in the south end of town, but it is maybe the best pho I've ever had. It's really good. It's a little hole-in-the-wall. My understanding is that the family leaves the country once a year for a month just to go buy ingredients in their homeland and bring them back. It's really, really special.

THRIFTING PARADISE

I'll give just a huge blanket endorsement of the **Peddlers Malls**. This is the first state I've lived in where you can actually type "Peddlers Mall" into your map, and five or six will pop up around town. And they're all like the same awesome consignment booths, where you wade through a million NASCAR blankets, and then suddenly there's this mid-century stuff that's really good. I probably furnished our entire house, including a Letterman print that was like ten bucks or whatever, and now those prints are major collector's items.

East

East Tennessee is something else. It has a particular magic to it where childhood fun is eternally in session for those ready to seize it. And even better, it has something different to offer in all seasons. So regardless of when the calendar finally lets you two sneak away for some good times, there is something joyful waiting for you. Choose your itinerary and get packing.

WINTER

Eat

A leisurely lunch at **Potchke** in Knoxville is anything but a waste of time—despite the name, which in Yiddish means to fuss around in the kitchen or dawdle. Here, taking your time is part of the charm, and trust me, you'll want to savor every bite. The pastel-hued dining room is a charming little daydream adding to the overall aura of comfort—which perfectly describes the food, too.

The menu is a deelish mix of Eastern European–inspired dishes that have folks lining up to order and then leaving five-star reviews by the hundreds. If

you're in the mood for something fresh and flavorful (other than your date, wink), the lox bialy sandwich is a crowd favorite with its fresh dill and a scallion schmear, snuggled in a pillowy bialy that'll have you wondering why you don't eat it every day. Or maybe you'll go for the borscht, a hearty beet soup that comes with warm garlic pampushki rolls, perfect for dipping and sopping up every last drop. Butttt let's not forget dessert. The chocolate babka is a must—rich, sweet, and topped with streusel. Pair it with a cup of coffee and you've got a sublime ending to your Potchke experience.

Stay

If you also had a life-changing experience at a Medieval Times at some point in your youth, you might want to consider packing up the family for a surprise weekend at the **Williamswood Castle** in Knoxville—a Scottish-inspired retreat that really goes for it. Built by Julia Tucker over the course of six years beginning in 1991, this 4,500-square-foot masterpiece has everything you need to feel like royalty from a time when health-

care involved leeches. Modeled on a hunting lodge from the old country, Williamswood welcomes you with a suit of armor guarding the entrance, and from that point on, every corner is packed with some kind of feudal flair.

As the lords and ladies of the estate, you can sip cocoa from the multilevel balcony over-looking the Tennessee River, lazily watching the water flow by. Inside it's time to get to work uncovering secrets, such as a book-shelf that swings open to expose a hidden staircase, or admire all the details such as a massive stained glass

window filling the home with colored light. And, because minimalism has yet to be invented in this world, the master bedroom's ceiling has a replica of the Sistine Chapel plus a dark carved wooden perch just begging for someone to dramatically shout, "Romeo, Romeo, wherefore art thou Romeo?" (We're mixing our eras, but you get the point.)

With riverfront access, ponds, and trees upon trees, it's easy to bundle up and occupy the fam in the great outdoors, but you're also tucked into three hundred acres of the **Ijams Nature Center**, meaning even more adventures await right outside your door. Most importantly: don't forget the secret passage to your very own pub where you can enjoy a fireside drink.

Do

We're not done with winter dates that feel like stepping into another realm, so head to **Anakeesta Mountaintop Adventure Park** in Gatlinburg to get high on life. Situated on a seventy-acre mountain, six hundred feet above the city, Anakeesta offers stunning views, especially from the **AnaVista Tower**, the highest point downtown with sweeping 360-degree views of the surrounding Smoky Mountains. But at this time of year, it's all about the holiday spirit— thousands of twinkling lights transform the park into a Christmas wonderland complete with festive entertainment. Even the Grinch would get into it.

For a bit of non-mistletoe-related adrenaline, don't miss the **Treetop Skywalk**, with 880 feet of hanging bridges that sway seemingly miles above the forest floor, offering lovers a bird's-eye view of the wintry landscape.

After all the holiday cheer coupled with the primal fear of being suspended in the air, make sure to experience the real showstopper: **Astra Lumina**. It's a mesmerizing night walk with a whole backstory that takes you through mysterious observatory grounds where the stars seem to have fallen from the sky just for you. The celestial pathway comes alive with shining lights, cosmic projections, and ethereal music that's all a little trippy. Your job is to connect with the stars (and each other) before they return to the sky above.

Now it's time to indulge the kid in us all, and that means grabbing your sled and heading to Knoxville's **Lakeshore Park**. This 185-acre gem is *the* go-to spot for sledding when the snow comes tumbling down. You'll know where to go by the sight of the hill that is dotted with kids in brightly knitted hats flinging themselves down the slopes with off-the-charts levels of excitement.

Find a good starting point at the top of the hill, and together, you and your partner can race down, feeling the rush of wind as you glide through the crisp winter air. Once you've had your fill of sledding thrills (and maybe a few friendly wipeouts), you can warm up with a thermos of hot cocoa and watch the kids continue the fun. If you can get into the joy enough to make you forget how cold your nose is, that's officially a success.

✱ ✱ ✱

For a hang that scratches the itch for both doomsdayers and history lovers (a winning combo for the right person!), take a trip to **Millennium Manor Castle** in Alcoa—an authentic stone fortress built in the 1930s. It had but one grand mission: to survive Armageddon and stand for one thousand years. That means you can't just craft any old castle; it was built to last, with outside walls at least twenty-five inches thick, interior walls nearly nineteen inches thick, and floors more than four feet thick. The 420-ton roof? A whopping three feet thick. Built by William Andrew Nicholson and his wife, Fair, the castle was single-handedly (double-handedly?) constructed over eight years without any modern machinery. Fair mixed and set the mortar while William built the structure that still stands today.

They weren't just after architectural achievement—they believed Armageddon would strike in 1959. When that year passed uneventfully, they pushed their doomsday prediction to 1969, guided by some religious numerology and other number crunching the IRS likely wouldn't trust. Now, decades later, the castle still looms large, a testament to their unwavering vision.

Meander through the grounds, taking in the oddity of a structure that's meant to withstand the test of time. Enclosed by a sturdy stone wall, the one-acre property is the perfect offbeat date for history buffs or those who simply appreciate the unusual—and perhaps a reminder that not all castles are built just for fairy tales.

SPRING

Eat

For a sweet and simple date, stop by **Donut Friar** in the **Village Shops**, a cozy spot that's been serving up fresh donuts daily since 1969. As soon as you walk in, the heavenly smell smacks you in the face, bending you to its will and making it impossible to resist ordering more than one. Nibble on raspberry powdered donuts, apple pillowy things, date bars, white cream pillows, or eclairs—it's all enough to blow your skirt up. The shop's old-school charm, including its kooky little statue of a friar holding a pile of donuts, adds to the experience. Just remember to come bearing cash in hand. The Friar doesn't know what Apple Pay is.

Stay

The time has come once again for us to talk about the legend herself: Dolly Parton. We begin with a stay at **Dollywood's DreamMore Resort and Spa**—a vacation cocktail of fun times and places to nap. You have all the requisite things needed to kick back—king-sized beds, a refreshing pool for a midday plunge, and all the other resort amenities to keep you comfy. But let's be real—it's all about being close to the **Dollywood** action. Whether you're planning on hitting the roller coasters, catching a show, or indulging in some sweet Southern treats, the resort is just minutes from the park, making it the ideal home base for your Dollywood adventures.

But if you're looking to go *big*, there's one splurge that takes the cake: **The Dolly Suite 1986**, aka Dolly Parton's former tour bus. Yes, for a cool *ten*

thousand dollars (with a two-night minimum), you can spend a couple of days in the place where Dolly herself lived while writing songs, working on projects, and traveling over 360 thousand miles from 2008 to 2022. It boasts three bunk beds instead of the standard six to make room for her wardrobe, a wig cabinet, and plenty of personalized touches. This Prevost bus was her beloved home on the road, and the interior decor—customized by Dolly—is a blinged-out reflection of her life during those years.

Do

We are by no means done talking about the Smoky Mountain Songbird. If you are into thrills, music, and pure joy, a trip to **Dollywood** is an absolute must. Located in Pigeon Forge, this park isn't just Tennessee's most visited attraction (with nearly three million visitors a year); it's a treasure trove of gleeful squeals, indulgent food, and entertainment galore.

First tip: Do not miss the **Thunderhead**. We know some coaster fans might dismiss wooden rides, but this isn't just any coaster—it's a wild, twisting masterpiece that leaves riders breathless. Trust me, it's worth every twist, turn, and scream. And while you're in adrenaline mode, hop on **Daredevil Falls**—a log flume ride that careens you over a waterfall, sending you plummeting down a sixty-foot drop at fifty miles per hour. Splash!

Between the rides (you gotta dry off so you don't slip on the next seat), take a break to enjoy one of the park's famous shows. Into bluegrass? Gospel? A whole lotta stuff in between? The live performances are crowd-pleasers for a reason. And *do not* leave without trying a potato tornado—a crispy, spiral-cut spud snack that's as fun to eat as it is to look at.

Every corner of this park is infused with the magic of Dolly Parton herself, from the butterfly-themed touches to the general good 'tude all around. Get swept away in the warm feelings. There won't be another like her ever again.

✳ ✳ ✳

If you love a date that blends history, class warfare, and a dash of 1990s cosplaying as 1910s cinematic nostalgia, cruise over to the **Titanic Museum Attraction**. Here you'll find a half-scale replica of the RMS Titanic sitting jauntily in the streets, offering museumgoers an immersive journey back to that fateful night in April 1912 when the British ocean liner struck an iceberg and sank on her maiden voyage. (And yes, we're all still wondering why Rose wouldn't share that door with Jack.)

Upon entry you'll receive a boarding pass representing an actual Titanic passenger or crew member. Moving through the museum and learning more about its history and people, you'll eventually discover the fate of your

passenger in the Titanic Memorial Room. Anyone who ever had a thing for young Leo DiCaprio will surely enjoy the replica of the Grand Staircase, which cost a cool million to reproduce, so take in every last detail.

For a chilling glimpse into the real-life experience of those onboard, sit in a full-size lifeboat and listen to true stories from survivors. It's a gut punch to connect the story we've all heard for so long that it sounds like a fable with the specific details of folks who fought for their lives. You won't think of the Unsinkable Ship the same way after this.

SUMMER

Eat

Time to head into a storybook and have some food. That means an afternoon at the **Wild Plum Tea Room**—a sweet little log cabin surrounded by flower gardens that are inspired by the tea houses of the Austrian mountains. Yes, it is as charming and homey as it sounds—like Grandma's kitchen meets mountain retreat, and all with a garden view.

The owners take pride in their dishes having an origin story. Their menu is culled from recipes passed down via word of mouth through grandmothers, aunts, uncles, neighbors, and artists, all of whom they call part of the "Wild Plum Family." That means early mornings when the crew make everything from scratch so it's all as fresh as can be. The food is worth the anticipation, but here's the catch: since it's all homemade, you'll need to make a reservation at least twenty-four hours in advance to snag a table to crunch a special salad or savor their famous wild plum tea.

Stay

Since time machines aren't available at Costco quite yet try checking into **The Wayback**, a vintage-inspired hotel that feels more Palm Springs than Tennessee. The heart of the property is **The Swim Club**—for all the loungey poolside vibes your soul needs. With a restored vintage Airstream bar serving up drinks and bites from lunch through the night, it's a darling spot to try out the nickname "Hollywood" on each other and unwind after bopping around town.

After five p.m., the vibe shifts to adults-only (which sounds slightly sexier than it's meant to), making it a laid-back, over-twenty-one hangout complete with a vast tequila selection for crafting the ultimate summer cocktail. It's all very summery, breezy, and exactly what you need for a relaxed getaway.

Do

For a sunrise date that's as breathtaking as it is exhilarating, snag tickets to the Smoky Mountain Sunrise Access at **Gatlinburg SkyPark**. Spots are limited, so it's truly an early bird gets the worm kind of sitch. It begins with a ride up the mountain on the iconic yellow SkyLift chairs, floating you to the summit of Crockett Mountain. The journey is cool, but so is the destination because

once you reach the top, get ready to stroll across the **SkyBridge**—the longest pedestrian suspension bridge in the world.

Spanning nearly seven hundred feet—which is not one, but *two* football fields—the bridge stretches over a deep valley, offering incredible views. At the midway point, brace yourself for the thirty feet of glass flooring that gives you a surreal, almost flying feeling as you look straight down with a dose of panic in your throat. If you're lucky you might even spot a black bear far below, curiously watching your sky-high feet.

As the sun slowly rises, casting golden light over the Smoky Mountains, you'll experience a heart-stopping mix of terror, thrill, and wonder—much like love itself (aww!).

✳ ✳ ✳

Alright, this date might actually be magic related. We're talking about witnessing the **synchronous fireflies of the Great Smoky Mountains**, a laser light show unlike any other because it's provided by nature. Every June thousands of fireflies put on a perfectly timed display akin to a drone firework show but without any of the tech. Imagine, if you will, six seconds of total darkness

followed by thousands of tiny lights flashing rapidly six times over three seconds and then darkness again. This cycle repeats over and over, creating a mesmerizing glowing dance club in the forest.

Experiencing this wonder takes some work and some luck. The easiest place and time to view this phenomenon is from the **Little River Trailhead** at Elkmont around the second week of June. There are trolleys running every few minutes from the **Sugarlands Visitor Center**, but beware of the one major caveat. There are but 1,800 parking spaces available and over 20,000 people aspiring to get one. Try your hand at luck by entering the parking lottery— snagging a spot feels like winning a golden ticket.

The incredible firefly display—discovered only in 1993—is actually part of the fireflies' mating ritual, with males flashing while flying and females responding from their stationary spots. It's a breathtaking show—watching these tiny boy creatures light up the night in perfect harmony to try and get the girl.

* * *

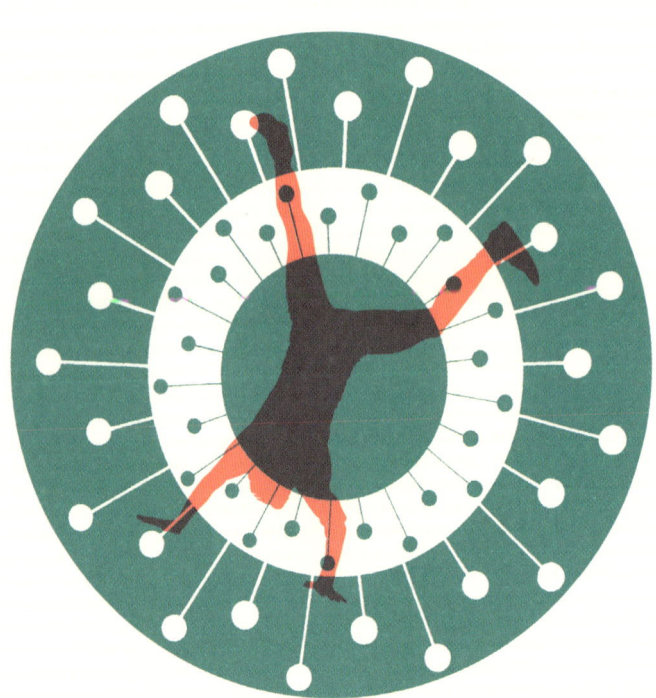

If you have the kind of partner who says, "Let's do something we've never done before," we've got you covered. Try a visit to **Outdoor Gravity Park**, the only zorbing park in the United States. Originally dreamed up by some adventurous folks in New Zealand, zorbing involves climbing into an eleven-foot inflatable ball and rolling down a thousand-foot hill—but with a twist. Inside the giant hamster ball, you'll find ten gallons of water, turning the whole thing into a whirling waterslide of sorts as you and your date slosh around inside.

As the ball rolls you'll stay relatively still in the water while the world spins around you, giving you the *impeccable* mix of adrenaline and giggle fits. Could this actually be the key to world peace? Think of what could happen if we get all the world leaders to agree to get into the zorb ball together. Figure that bit out when you're in there, will you?

FALL

Eat

Sometimes you're in the mood for the classics, and for that, ramble on over to the **Log Cabin Pancake House**, where you'll find exactly what the name promises: a charming log cabin full of pancakes. Inside, the wagon wheel chandeliers and giant rock fireplace give off rustic, homey vibes, while carafes of coffee keep your cup full all morning. It's the kind of place where families—from children to grandparents—are happily devouring scrambled eggs, waffles, and all things syrupy.

With over fifty years of serving up breakfast goodness, this spot has perfected the art of comfort food. Be sure to try the Cabin Special—buckwheat pancakes topped with crushed pineapple, hot syrup, and whipped margarine—a sugary hug of sorts.

Stay

Looking for a pretty leaf-turning-viewing relaxing escape? Opt for **Creekside Hideaway** in the Smoky Mountains—a collection of adorable tiny homes nestled in nature, complete with two creeks and a serene two-acre fishing pond. Each cabin offers rustic charm with modern comforts, including fire pits, BBQs, and big ol' rocking chairs where you can sip your morning coffee or enjoy a quiet moment.

Located near everything from horseback riding and moonshine tasting to theme parks and mini golf, the area has plenty of fun ways to fill your days. But if you're looking to simply unwind and . . . be, your cozy cabin is a splendid place to focus on each other. Play a lengthy board game that you wouldn't normally have time for, steal a few kisses, read a new favorite book, and let the peaceful surroundings work their magic. When the evening hits, crack open all

the s'mores fixin's. With firelight flickering and the sounds of the creek nearby, settle in and relax, all while roasting marshmallows and reconnecting with your favorite person.

Do

After a day exploring the Smokies, unwind in one of Creekside Hideaway's exclusive **wood-fired hot tub boats**—available only to cabin guests. How's this for a day date? A two-hour rental where you and your sweet pea relax in 105-degree warmth, gently floating around a private lake. The boat is equipped with an adjustable electric motor so you can effortlessly glide along while surrounded by nature. With firewood and ice already stocked, all you have to do is enjoy the moment. And when your luxurious soak is over, you can even get a cart ride back to your cabin—because after floating to a perfect state of chill, why not indulge in one more little luxury?

For a perfect spooky-season date (are we still saying spooky season?), head to the **Elkmont Ghost Town**, a once-thriving getaway now filled with abandoned cabins waiting to be explored. Elkmont Historic District was Tennessee's answer to the Hamptons from 1910 to 1935, where Knoxville's wealthy would escape by train for weekends in the mountains. At its peak there were eighty-one cabins where fancy couples spent their summers, and now you and your partner can wander through what's left of that old glamour.

It's free to explore and there are park rangers around if you want the inside scoop on the town's history. As you wander through the decaying cabins, it's easy to imagine the elegant gatherings of yesteryear, with couples cuddling up just like you are now.

✳ ✳ ✳

Today is a bit of nature's wonder with a splash of history and maybe a touch of 1990s rave vibes. We're talking, of course, about **Forbidden Caverns**, one of Tennessee's most fascinating underground attractions. With over 8,350 caves registered, Tennessee boasts more caves than any other state, and this one is a must-see. As you venture deeper, you'll be wowed by sparkling formations, towering natural chimneys, and zones with names like the "Grotto of Evil Spirits." A crystal-clear stream runs through the cave, adding to the sense of *oooooooooooooooooooo*.

The colorful lighting effects give it a bit of an underground club vibe, so while you might be the only one spontaneously breaking into dance, surely the other cavegoers will at least understand. The place is also home to some pretty freaking cool calcite formations, which are still growing, in addition to the largest wall of rare cave onyx (aka dripstones) known to exist.

So it might not actually be an underground club, but the caverns do have some wild-party-related history. From the 1920s to 1943, it served as a secret spot for moonshiners who took advantage of the constant water supply and isolation to whip up homemade whiskey. Something to remember as you stroll through this underground marvel: you're also walking in the footsteps of the Smoky Mountain's bootlegging past. Cheers!

JESSICA CARR is the owner of **Girls Gotta Eat Good**, the first Asian-owned bakery in Knoxville, known and loved for her purple ube crinkle cookies, as well as other fabulous Filipino treats. She is also the cofounder of the town's AAPI Business Association. *GirlsGottaEatGood.com*

FOR A TREAT-FILLED SATURDAY

The **Market Square Farmers Market** in the very center of downtown Knoxville is really great. There's **Pastelito's Cuban Bakery**. They have guava and cheese pastries, which are really, really good. A Chinese bakery called **GraceCakeUS**, which opened after I started, makes traditional moon cakes. And there is **Rainbow Roots Floral Co.** They do bouquets that are great. You can get flowers *and* then you can get treats.

FOR FILM BUFFS

We have a local independent theater called **Central Cinema**, located on Central Street, and they do a lot of showings of cult classic movies. They also host a horror film festival every year. We love going there, and the people who run it are amazing. It's really nice having an independent movie theater. I saw *Purple Rain*, which, obviously, is a Prince concert, which is great, but the movie's narrative is so crazy.

FOR CAFFEINE AND CULTURE

My favorite coffee shop in Knoxville is **South Press Café**. It is trans owned, and Joslynn has helped me so much. She allowed me to do pop-ups in her coffee shop when I first started and didn't charge me anything. She's doing amazing things for the queer community in Knoxville. She's created a safe space for people to go, and the coffee shop's vibe is cool. The drinks are amazing and they source their treats and bagels from local bakers. They also host drag shows and nighttime events, so it's a really great sober queer space.

A DINNER GO-TO SPOT

We have a place called **Gogi Korean Kitchen**, and the owners are amazing. My fiancé actually proposed to me there. It's really beautiful on the inside—nothing too fancy, just a nice restaurant. They do lots of traditional Korean food, like bulgogi, which comes out on a sizzling hot plate, and banchan, the little side dishes that go with everything. They also have wings. All the food is amazing; we go all the time.

CATFISH QUEEN

A lunch spot that I love going to is **Jackie's Dream**. It's Black owned, and she makes soul food. And no matter where we go, no matter where we travel to, and even places that are known for having super, super good southern food, Jackie's Dream is always my favorite. I've never had better fried catfish anywhere else. And I have family that live in Louisiana, and I've been to New Orleans and Baton Rouge. I've traveled all over the South my entire life, and her catfish is the best.

South

A weekend in Chattanooga is pure southern charm, so we went through the effort of detailing a no-brainer itinerary for you, leaving you with the sole task of having fun. Step into the glamorous train life at the historic Chattanooga Choo Choo, where vintage rail cars evoke golden-age travel vibes. Wander through the iconic Rock City with stunning views and whimsical paths. Indulge in belt-busting meals at local eateries with hearty fare. And sleep like a baby, away from it all for a couple of days.

NIGHT 1

Scoot out of work early if you can and make it to town in time for a blissful, adults-only dinner at **The Rosecomb**, where you can sip creative cocktails and indulge in flavor-bursting small plates. The 1920s cottage setting is adorable, especially when you grab a seat in the garden under the striped umbrellas and twinkly lights. Try the deviled eggs with hot honey or the Florist Gump cocktail, a delightful mix of honeysuckle vodka, lime, grapefruit, cava, and a hint of salt.

After dinner, stroll over to **The Hotel Chalet** for a night of romantic luxury. Situated at the

heart of Chattanooga's Choo Choo district, this recently renovated gem features train cars, which have been transformed into dreamy rooms with velvet furniture, teal walls, and all the modern amenities you could want. Whether you're unwinding in your stately room or exploring the nearby Station Street for a nightcap, the hotel is one to remember with its century of history and thirst for glamour.

DAY 2

Start your day with a delectable breakfast just steps from your hotel at **Niedlov's Bakery & Cafe**. Walk into the little brick bakery, where the warm, homey smell of fresh-baked goods wraps around you like a hug. We've got a full day ahead, so try the simple breakfast, featuring a fluffy omelet with creamy Boursin cheese, all wrapped up in a buttery, flaky croissant that's been baked fresh that same morning.

After breakfast, head to the iconic **Rock City**—a natural wonder packed with incredible sights. Wander through massive ancient rock formations and gardens with over four hundred native plant species. There's the panoramic "See Seven States" view where, you guessed it, they claim that on a clear day you can see Tennessee, Kentucky, Virginia, South Carolina, North Carolina, Georgia, and Alabama. But the fun really starts on the 4,100-foot **Enchanted Trail**, where you'll crunch through sections like Fat Man's Squeeze and Needle's Eye, both of which force you to shuffle sideways through narrow rock crevices. (American treasure and Chattanooga boy Leslie Jordan once declared, "Life is fine if I can get through the Fat Man's Squeeze.")

Of course you'll stop by Lover's Leap, a spot with sweeping views perfect for a romantic kiss and a photo op to prove you had the romantic kiss. After exploring the nooks and crannies of the trail, you'll soon find yourself in Fairyland Caverns, where larger-than-life dioramas of childhood fairy tales glow in retro neon colors. There's nothing like a glowing Rip Van Winkle to get the day's energy really flowing.

Before you wrap up your adventure, be sure to add a visit to the **Incline Railway**, a funicular system that's been running for over 125 years. The ride up Lookout Mountain is a thrilling way to take in more stunning views. The railway's history is fascinating, too—originally made of wood and powered by coal-burning steam engines, it now uses two hundred-horsepower motors to power the cable. Over the decades it's seen its fair share of famous riders—Teddy Roosevelt took a trip in 1905, during his presidency, and Elizabeth Taylor followed in the 1950s. Now it's your turn to join the ranks!

At the bottom Incline station in St. Elmo, you'll find an array of special local spots. You can explore microbrewery tours, homemade candle-making, and fresh flowers, or you can grab a bite at one of the many little bistros or have a drink on an outdoor patio. If you're up for more activity, there's an indoor climbing wall, or you might call the action of lifting hand-dipped ice cream to and from your lips an activity, too.

Once you've finally done all your walking and made your way back to town, end your day with a delicious dinner at **Ernest Chinese**, where the vibe is a modern mix of industrial chic and natural wood, accented by stunning cherry blossom installations that greet you as you walk in. Dive into a feast of chewy dumplings, garlicky lo mein noodles, and spicy green beans—each dish a bit better than the last. Don't worry about the garlic breath; it's a nonissue when you're both partaking of the vampire repellent. Plus brushing your teeth side by side later on could be considered an act of foreplay.

Afterward, take a leisurely stroll back to your room. Not quite ready to call it a night? Pop into one of the cute on-site bars for a nightcap. After all, it's your vacation—why not savor one more drink to toast a perfect day together?

DAY 3

Start your morning with a breakfast burrito on the expansive patio at **The Daily Ration**, where you can sip your coffee and gulp the fresh morning air. After fueling up, it's time to hit the **dance steps on Frazier Avenue**—a quirky little spot where you can't help but feel like breaking into a twirl or two. Near the entrance to Coolidge Park, sweep your lovebug over to see the sidewalks on Frazier. Why? You'll find dance steps embedded in the pavement. From the rumba to the merengue to the hokey pokey, there are diagrams on the ground to show you how to swing each other around. Fellas, trust us on this one.

Next mosey into **Coolidge Park**, a peaceful riverside escape with loads to offer a couple out for an afternoon. Be sure to hop onto the **1894 Dentzel antique carousel**—for just one dollar you get an old-fashioned ride surrounded by fifty-two beautifully hand-carved animals, a charming calliope band organ, and ornate gold-leaf benches. And if that's not enough to induce some nostalgic feelings, take a moment to watch the kids play in the giant fountain, laughter filling the air. Even if it sounds a little corny, hold hands, take a deep breath, and appreciate the beauty of this shared moment and the life you have together.

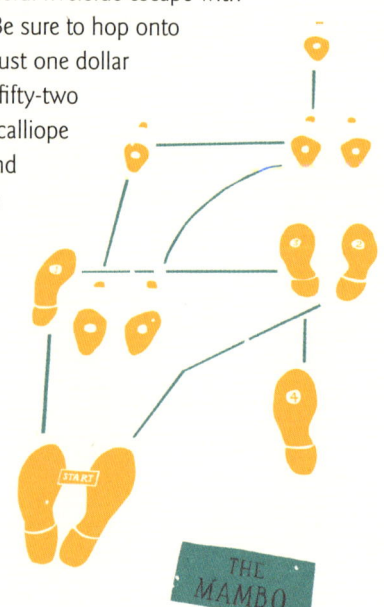

THE MAMBO

West

Memphis is a soulful city with an eclectic mix of things to do. We're talking kooky, sky-high pyramids, diving into the powerful stories at the National Civil Rights Museum and Stax, and scoping out Victorian mansions. It's catching the elegant marching ducks at the Peabody Hotel and taking in Graceland, the iconic home of Elvis. Plus live music abounds, including the spot where the blues began.

BASS PLAYER

Editor's note: You do not need to be outdoorsy in any way to partake in the next date. In fact looking at all the whoosits and whatsits on display at this wild **Bass Pro Shops Pyramid** when you have no clue what they are might make your visit even more entertaining. It's akin to looking at medieval gadgets and wondering if they're torture devices or something for cooking. The giant pyramid (not as old as the ones in Egypt for the non-history folks among us) is a hotel with far too much taxidermy for animal lovers to feel comfortable. The rooms look onto the shop, which includes a myriad of oddities for a retail location, such as six hundred thousand gallons of water features with creatures swimming about, a full cypress swamp with hundred-foot-tall trees and alligator pools, and an interactive wetlands education center. You know! Normal boutique stuff. When you're done looking at all the *waves hand at everything*, pop up to **The Lookout** at the top of the Pyramid for a drink three hundred feet above the Mississippi River.

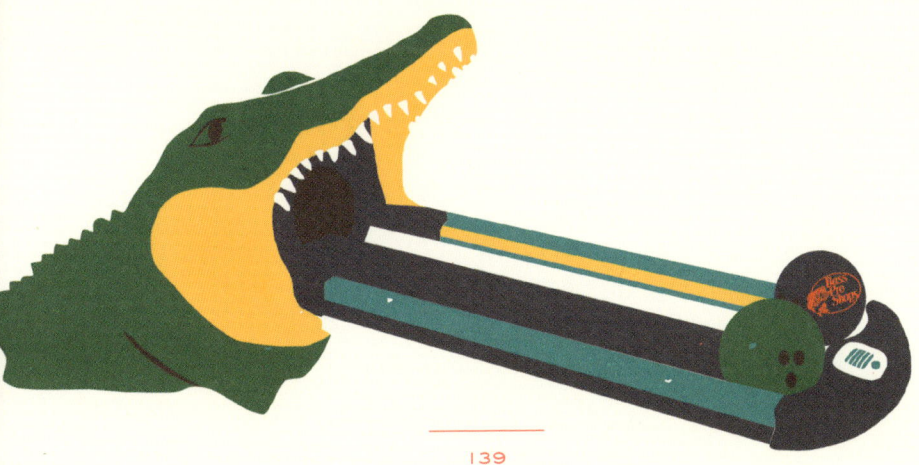

THE MORE
YOU KNOW

Start your date with a powerful and moving visit to the **National Civil Rights Museum**, built around the historic Lorraine Motel, the site where Dr. Martin Luther King Jr. was assassinated in 1968. The museum traces the civil rights movement in the United States, from the horrors of slavery to the ongoing fight for justice today. With immersive exhibits, such as life-size statues, large-scale historical photos, and oral histories, you'll dive deep into significant moments such as *Brown v. Board of Education*, voting rights struggles, and the marches

that shaped the nation. It's an experience that brings history to life and leaves a lasting impact—making it no wonder that it's ranked in the top 5 percent of US museums on Tripadvisor.

Just a five-minute walk away, keep the convo going over a refreshment with a stop at **Earnestine & Hazel's**, a dive bar steeped in history and character. Once connected to a local music joint that saw the likes of B.B. King, Tina Turner, and Aretha Franklin (who came over post show to hang out), the bar claims to have the greatest jukebox in the country, and with that kind of music legacy, it's easy to believe. If you're feeling brave, you can even explore its reputation as one of the most haunted places in America. Order a simple Soul Burger and a local beer and soak in the storied atmosphere where legends once drank, laughed, and surely someone snuck a kiss or two.

JUST DUCKY

For this one we're donning our fancy pants to feel the elegance of yesteryear. Let's say you've booked a room at the historic **The Peabody Memphis** hotel. In addition to the stately place to snuggle at night, opulent ceilings, and intricate woodwork, you'll also get to see the famous **Duck March**.

It started in 1933 when a handful of ducks were placed in the hotel's pretty fountain. A few years later a former animal circus trainer, Edward Pembroke, came on board to care for the ducks, and he taught them to strut down the red carpet each day to their signature song, with fans gathered

on either side to cheer them on. All these decades later you can still watch the latest generation of duckies walk the red carpet every day. And if you're dying to know what they do in the hours they're not in the lobby, the answer is that they hang out in their Royal Duck Palace on the hotel's rooftop—a two-hundred-thousand-dollar marble and glass structure, complete with a tiny replica of the hotel. Cue the theme song to *DuckTales*!

Clearly we're off to a high-rolling start, but let's valiantly march on with a visit to **Victorian Village**. Once named Millionaire's Row, the area is full of gorgeous Victorian mansions built between 1845 and 1890 when a bunch of Richie Riches all set up shop here. Take a tour around whatever flavor of grandeur scratches your itch, from twenty-five-room Italianate mansions to pre-Civil War Greek Revival numbers to haunted Victorian staircases. End the day with a highfalutin cocktail at the beautiful Mollie Fontaine Taylor House, now known as **Mollie Fontaine Lounge**, where the reigning motto is, "If one kind of decoration is good, two or three kinds will be better." This means you can sip your grand concoction while flirting from a tufted couch surrounded by gorgeous stained glass accents and chandeliers aplenty, thinking about how couples 150 years ago were doing the same.

LOVE ME TENDER

Curl that lip up, swing that pelvis around, and head off to **Graceland**, the iconic home-turned-museum of Elvis Presley. Despite the fact that Elvis "left the building" nearly fifty years ago, the crowds have not dwindled. It's the second most visited house in the United States after the White House, and stepping inside feels like you're entering a 1977 time capsule. From the Jungle Room's shag carpet to the retro kitchen and living spaces, every corner oozes vintage charm, with the King's maximalist personality felt throughout the mansion.

Once you've explored Graceland, don't miss the two-hundred-thousand-square-foot **Elvis Presley's Memphis** complex just a short walk away. Here you'll find an astonishing collection of Elvis's famous jumpsuits, sparkly enough to earn drag queen approval. Add

STAX

SOULSVILLE
USA

to that the Presidential Medal of Freedom that shows just how far Elvis's influence reached. From his custom cars to gold records, this immersive experience offers a closer look at the life of the King, making it a good spot for history buffs, nostalgia lovers, and those obsessed with Austin Butler's Elvis voice.

HOT TIP: Each year Team Graceland pulls out all of Elvis's original Christmas decorations, such as twinkly blue lights and a vintage Santa lawn decoration, for those who love the King and Christmas.

We're not done celebrating music in any way, so it's off to the **Stax Museum of American Soul Music**, which is fully dedicated to the legacy of American soul music. Nestled inside the original **Stax Records** studio, it's the place to go to see ancient recording consoles, walls of the sexiest albums of all time (which honestly includes anything by Otis Redding), and glamorous stage costumes. It's far from an uptight museum experience, with a full "Express Yourself" dancefloor accompanied by vintage episodes of *Soul Train* playing next to it. Google that reference if you don't get it, and you're welcome in advance. Finally you must see the pièce de résistance: Isaac Hayes's (who won an Oscar for creating the iconic *Shaft* theme song) custom Cadillac Eldorado that he got in a full Treat Yo' Self sitch after renegotiating his deal with Stax in 1972. It's fully glammed out to all levels with a TV, a fridge, twenty-four-carat gold exterior trim, and white floorboards.

Now that you're in the dancing mood, end the day with a visit to the iconic **Beale Street**—a National Historic Landmark known for its legendary live music with the greats, such as Memphis Minnie and B.B. King. Its three neon-lit blocks are chock-full of nightclubs with live music, places to snag vacay memories, and spots to grab food. Long a hub for Black-owned businesses, it became the epicenter of blues music as we know it, with W.C. Handy, known as the "Father of the Blues," playing from this very street.

Acknowledgments

For hot tips and decades of friendship, The Watson Twins and Jenny Lewis, and Portia Sabin and Slim Moon. We are forever inspired by your contributions to Nashville and the music world at large. To all the Nashvillians whose paths we crossed on our visits and who pointed us to their favorite spots, we are especially grateful for your generous guidance. To our special field experts, Ashley Currie, Danny Seim, Jessica Carr, and Chandra and Leigh Watson, both the readers and we thank you for sharing your wisdom.

To our chosen families, who keep us anchored when we're being battered by life's many storms: Matty, David, Sydney and Milo, Tymberly, Danny, Fritz, and Golden, Emma, Amy, and Jude (who was delivered during the last weeks of writing this book!). We love you and can't wait to be laughing with you soon!

To our beloved Sasquatch family: thanks for helping nurture yet another one of these weird books into the world. Especially to Jen Worick, who helped sculpt the shape of the Book of Dates enterprise; Jill Saginario, who picked up the torch and continues to run with it headlong into the future; and Tony Ong for his exquisite eye in the final months leading up to print.

As always, a *gigantic* debt of gratitude to Heather Brooks Rensmith, our couple's therapist, for listening, reflecting, and reminding us to listen and reflect ourselves. We'll figure it out one of these days. JK, we gotta keep you in business!

For forever influencing our explorations, a vociferous shout-out to the regional journalists and local publications that keep us in the loops that matter most. And to the content creators and TikTokers whose stories seeped into our everyday lives: your hard work and dedication do not go unappreciated.

Cheat Sheet

> **A HANDY GUIDE FOR FINDING THE BEST DATE FOR YOU**

Index

About the Authors

EDEN DAWN is a Guinness World Record holder, an award-winning journalist, a Pacific Northwest Booksellers Association–bestselling author, a veteran stylist for bands and fashion editorials, and a sequin-wearing lady with a microphone from Portland, Oregon. Known as a "Fun Expert," you can often see her performing at storytelling events, moderating panels, chatting through live television segments, emceeing galas, and hosting her own quarterly *Fashion in Film* series.

ASHOD SIMONIAN is creative director and cofounder of Imaginary Authors, a niche perfume house, and author of *Real Fun*, a book of photography and stories documenting his decade spent touring the world in various indie rock bands.

Together Eden and Ashod first began publishing the *Book of Dates* series in 2021 as a natural extension of their adventurous, overextended lifestyle, bringing together Eden's passion for words and Ashod's hand-crafted illustrations. They met backstage at a friend's rock show in 2012 and were married in 2017 in Joshua Tree, California. Every day that they get to do what they do side by side is a gift they don't take for granted.

They live in a slightly creaky one-hundred-year-old house with their two cats, Daphne and Foxglove, surrounded by plants.